Financial Literacy
Lessons & Activities

Grade 4

Writing: Bryan Langdo
Content Editing: Kathleen Jorgensen
Copy Editing: Cathy Harber
Art Direction: Yuki Meyer
Cover Design: Yuki Meyer
Illustration: Dana Regan
Design/Production: Paula Acojido
Yuki Meyer
Jessica Onken

EMC 3124

Visit
teaching-standards.com
to view a correlation
of this book.

**Correlated to
Current Standards**

**Congratulations on your purchase of some of the
finest teaching materials in the world.**

*Photocopying the pages in this book
is permitted for <u>single-classroom use only</u>.
Making photocopies for additional classes
or schools is prohibited.*

For information about other Evan-Moor products, call 1-800-777-4362,
fax 1-800-777-4332, or visit our website, www.evan-moor.com.
Entire contents © 2022 Evan-Moor Corporation
10 Harris Court, Suite C-3, Monterey, CA 93940-5773. Printed in USA.

CPSIA: Sheridan Saline, Inc., Saline, MI, USA [9/2023]

Why Teach Financial Literacy?

Preparing students to understand financial concepts in school and in the real world includes teaching them about money and giving them the information that they need to be informed consumers. The foundational concepts of earning, buying, saving, and borrowing can be taught at the earliest grade levels, when children start developing habits with money. The concepts of investing and protecting money can be introduced a few years later.

For many people, transactions frequently happen electronically through tap-and-go technology in stores, online shopping, and electronic funds transfers to pay bills. Some children may rarely see actual money changing hands. This may mean that they have less opportunity to connect money's value to the things it buys. Handling bills and coins, even if they are play money, gives children a concrete understanding of how we use money to get other things of value.

Having information about how the financial world works helps people make appropriate decisions for themselves to meet their own needs and goals. Young adults need to be prepared before stepping fully into an adult's world, where there are so many risks for making mistakes with money. While people's choices are personal and may vary widely from one person to the next, everyone must find a way to navigate through a variety of financial structures.

As you present financial concepts to students, consider their diverse backgrounds and their varying world views, encouraging them to form their own opinions and share their ideas about spending, saving, credit, and more. As students grow and change, their approach to financial literacy concepts and skills may also change. It is important to provide them the tools they need so they can make the best decisions for themselves and to empower them with a solid foundation to become informed consumers who have their own financial identities.

Contents

Reproducible Student Resource/Reference Pages

Units

Financial Concepts: All choices have an "opportunity cost": the options you don't choose.
Buyers prioritize or rank what they want.
Buyers should consider cost vs. benefit (is it worth what you're paying?).

Math Skills: addition, subtraction, multiplication, division, currency

Financial Concepts: Different jobs require different skills.
Employers pay what they think the skills are worth.

Math Skills: addition, subtraction, multiplication, division, graphs, currency

Financial Concepts: A budget is a plan for earning and spending money.
Income must always be at least as high as expenses.

Math Skills: addition, subtraction, multiplication, division, fractions, currency

Financial Concepts: Individual people and businesses have their own accounts at banks.
Banks have many services, including savings accounts, checking accounts, and lending money.
Banks charge money for their services.

Math Skills: addition, subtraction, multiplication, currency

What's in *Financial Literacy Lessons and Activities*

Financial Literacy Lessons and Activities lets students get hands-on with personal finance. Based on national standards from the Council for Economic Education and the Jump Start Coalition, these lessons and activities make using money concrete for students in real-life situations.

10 Engaging Units

Financial Literacy Lessons and Activities offers 10 units on grade-level topics involving the use of money. Each unit's topic focuses on where money is spent, what money is spent on, how to receive money, or how to handle money responsibly. Each unit brings together vocabulary and financial concepts using a story and explicit instruction. Practice includes math application and an engaging activity.

Unit Features

Units are designed to fit into a weekly lesson plan. Each reproducible 12-page unit provides information for the teacher, a story or dialogue, vocabulary, concept practice, math application, and an activity.

Teacher Overview

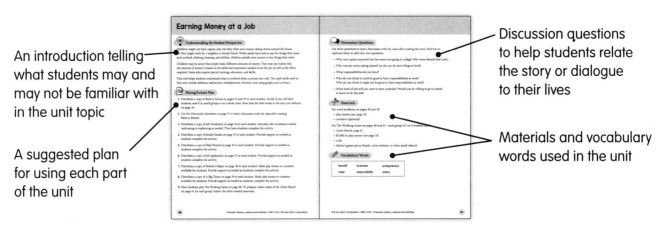

An introduction telling what students may and may not be familiar with in the unit topic

A suggested plan for using each part of the unit

Discussion questions to help students relate the story or dialogue to their lives

Materials and vocabulary words used in the unit

Story or Dialogue

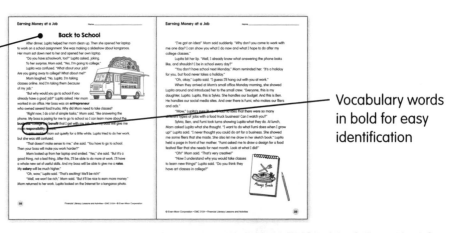

A two-page fiction text that introduces the topic in context, as well as the vocabulary that students will learn

Vocabulary words in bold for easy identification

Vocabulary and Concept Practice

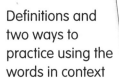

Definitions and two ways to practice using the words in context

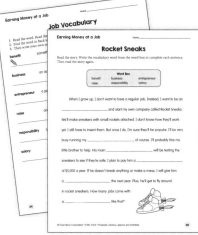

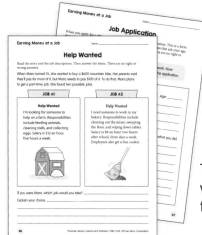

Two open-ended ways to practice the concept

Math Application

Scenarios using money-based word problems; manipulatives and other aids provided

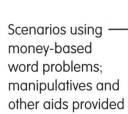

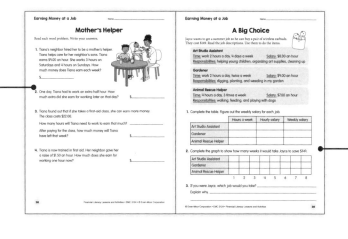

Scaffolding provided for multistep problems

Activity

A fun art activity, game, role-play, or other activity that lets students practice using money in the unit's context

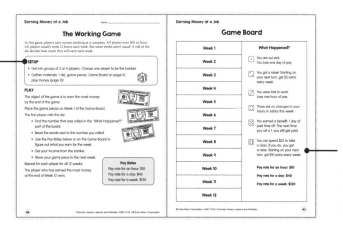

Cutouts, fill-in table, and game cards or game board provided

Cutouts, reference sheets, and other aids support student learning through all units:

Play money dollar bills to use as manipulatives and in games

Multiply to 100 table to help with math facts

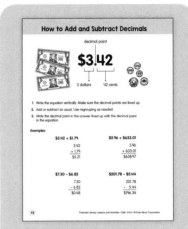

Steps for how to **add and subtract decimals with examples**

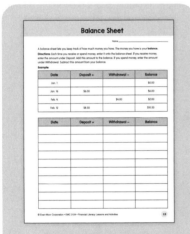

A **balance sheet** form to help students keep track of running totals

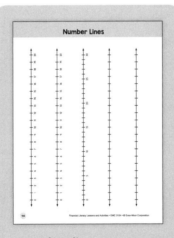

Number lines to support skip counting and repeated adding (multiplication)

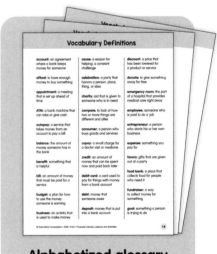

Alphabetized glossary of all vocabulary words in the book

Answer Key

Answers are provided for the Vocabulary and Math Application pages. The correct answer or a sample response is shown unless the question is completely open-ended.

How to Use *Financial Literacy Lessons and Activities*

Support for Consumers-to-Be

Encourage students to relate the concepts and experiences they read about to their own lives. Be mindful not to judge their choices or habits and to respect cultural and family attitudes toward using money. Tell them how money works, not how they should or shouldn't use it.

Key Words

As you decide which, if not all, of the pages in each unit you will reproduce for your students, be sure to include the unit vocabulary page that defines key concept terms. This page is useful throughout the unit. Have students tape it to their desks for easy reference. If you send a page home for homework, also send the unit vocabulary page for support.

The Importance of Discussion

There is no one right way to earn, spend, or save money. Facilitate student discussions so that they can share ideas, thoughts, and habits. Learning from others' successes and struggles improves planning and problem-solving skills.

Connections to Other Subjects

The units in this book provide opportunities to describe characters, identify sequence and cause and effect, and increase vocabulary (reading/language arts). The units augment learning about different people's needs and wants, how a community works together, and taking responsibility (social studies). The word problems let students practice handling money, basic arithmetic, and reasoning (math).

Keeping It Playful

Use play money frequently. Consider having a good supply of play money ready before starting to use the book and collecting it after each lesson to use throughout the year. The activities at the ends of the units provide opportunities for students to work together, use hands-on materials, make decisions for themselves, and often create something meaningful.

For Non-U.S. Classrooms

While this book uses U.S. coins and bills, it can be used in any country. If your country's main denomination is not the dollar, substitute *euro, yuan, pound, rupee, riyal,* or whatever is appropriate along with your equivalent of *cent.* Practicing one-to-many correspondence is still useful for students, as are the decision-making and reasoning challenges provided.

Play Money Cutouts

Multiply to 100 Table

✕	0	1	2	3	4	5	6	7	8	9	10
0	0	0	0	0	0	0	0	0	0	0	0
1	0	1	2	3	4	5	6	7	8	9	10
2	0	2	4	6	8	10	12	14	16	18	20
3	0	3	6	9	12	15	18	21	24	27	30
4	0	4	8	12	16	20	24	28	32	36	40
5	0	5	10	15	20	25	30	35	40	45	50
6	0	6	12	18	24	30	36	42	48	54	60
7	0	7	14	21	28	35	42	49	56	63	70
8	0	8	16	24	32	40	48	56	64	72	80
9	0	9	18	27	36	45	54	63	72	81	90
10	0	10	20	30	40	50	60	70	80	90	100

How to Add and Subtract Decimals

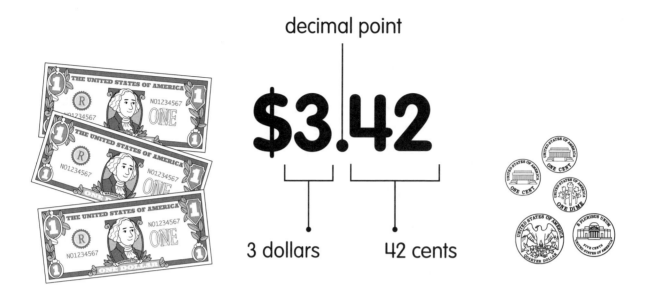

decimal point

$3.42

3 dollars   42 cents

1. Write the equation vertically. Make sure the decimal points are lined up.

2. Add or subtract as usual. Use regrouping as needed.

3. Write the decimal point in the answer lined up with the decimal point in the equation.

Examples:

$3.42 + $1.79

$$\begin{array}{r} 3.42 \\ + 1.79 \\ \hline \$5.21 \end{array}$$

$5.96 + $633.01

$$\begin{array}{r} 5.96 \\ + 633.01 \\ \hline \$638.97 \end{array}$$

$7.30 − $6.82

$$\begin{array}{r} 7.30 \\ - 6.82 \\ \hline \$0.48 \end{array}$$

$201.78 − $5.44

$$\begin{array}{r} 201.78 \\ - 5.44 \\ \hline \$196.34 \end{array}$$

Financial Literacy Lessons and Activities • EMC 3124 • © Evan-Moor Corporation

Balance Sheet

Name _____

A balance sheet lets you keep track of how much money you have. The money you have is your **balance**.

Directions: Each time you receive or spend money, enter it onto the balance sheet. If you receive money, enter the amount under Deposit. Add this amount to the balance. If you spend money, enter the amount under Withdrawal. Subtract this amount from your balance.

Example:

Date	Deposit +	Withdrawal –	Balance
Jan. 1			$0.00
Jan. 16	$6.00		$6.00
Feb. 4		$4.00	$2.00
Feb. 12	$8.50		$10.50

Date	Deposit +	Withdrawal –	Balance

Number Lines

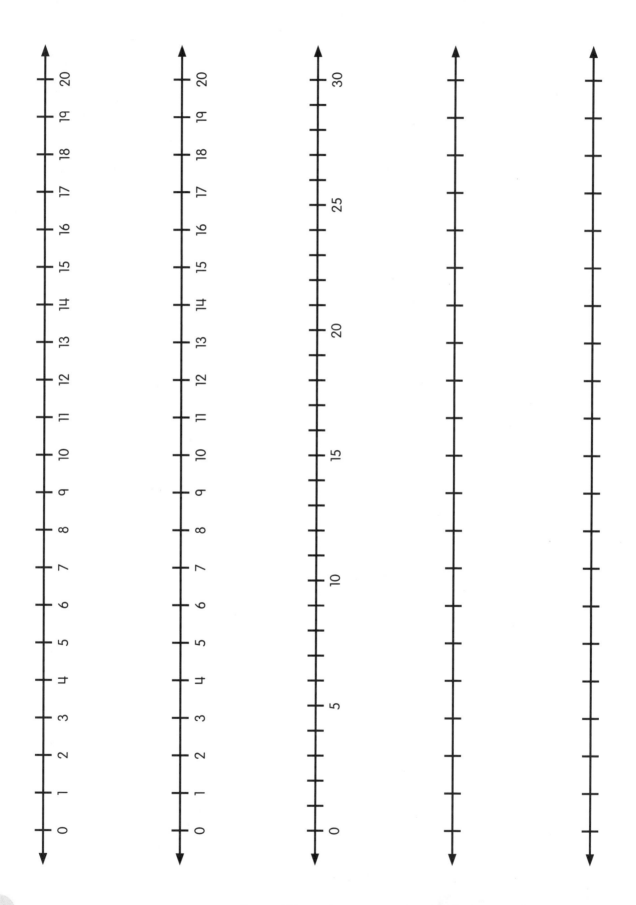

 Financial Literacy Lessons and Activities • EMC 3124 • © Evan-Moor Corporation

Vocabulary Definitions

account: an agreement where a bank keeps money for someone

afford: to have enough money to buy something

appointment: a meeting that is set up ahead of time

ATM: a bank machine that can take or give cash

autopay: a service that takes money from an account to pay a bill

balance: the amount of money someone has in the bank

benefit: something that is helpful

bill: an amount of money that must be paid for a service

budget: a plan for how to use the money someone is earning

business: an activity that is used to make money

cause: a reason for helping; a constant challenge

celebration: a party that honors a person, place, thing, or idea

charity: aid that is given to someone who is in need

compare: to look at how two or more things are different and alike

consumer: a person who buys goods and services

copay: a small charge for a doctor visit or medicine

credit: an amount of money that can be spent now and paid back later

debit card: a card used to pay for things with money from a bank account

debt: money that someone owes

deposit: money that is put into a bank account

discount: a price that has been lowered for a product or service

donate: to give something away for free

emergency room: the part of a hospital that provides medical care right away

employee: someone who is paid to do a job

entrepreneur: a person who starts his or her own business

expense: something you pay for

favors: gifts that are given out at a party

food bank: a place that collects food for people who need it

fundraiser: a way to collect money for something

goal: something a person is trying to do

Vocabulary Definitions, *continued*

homeless: not having an indoor place to live

host: someone who has a party

insurance: a service that helps pay expensive bills

interest: money made by lending money or paid to borrow money

invitation: a note asking someone to come to a party

limit: the highest amount allowed

manage: to handle something in a successful way

minimum: the smallest amount

monthly: happening once a month

mortgage: a loan that someone gets to buy a house

need: something that a person must have

organization: a group that works together to do something

prefer: to like one thing more than another

prescription: a note from a doctor for a specific medicine

prioritize: to figure out what is important and what is not

procedure: any treatment done to help fix an injury or illness

product: something that is made and then sold

profit: the amount of money left over after buying supplies and paying workers

purchase: to buy something

quantity: an amount or a number

raise: an increase in how much money a worker is paid

receipt: a paper that shows what you bought and how much you paid

rent: money paid every month to use something owned by someone else

responsibility: a duty or a task that someone is supposed to do

risk: the possibility of losing something or being harmed

salary: the money that a worker is paid

statement: a report that tells how much money has been used

subscribe: to sign up for and receive an information or entertainment service

surgery: fixing the body by cutting into it

teller: a person who works in a bank at the counter

therapy: treatment to rebuild strength and ability

transaction: a trade of goods or services for money

utility: a service, such as power or water, that a household needs

volunteer: a person who does a task without getting paid

want: something that a person would like to have

waste management: a service that collects garbage and recycling

withdraw: to take out

Buying at the Store

 Understanding the Student Perspective

Children often have some experience buying things. Stores make products look attractive, and children make choices based on a variety of reasons. They may not realize that the same items can differ in price from store to store or that similar items can have different features.

Children may see their parents using electronic forms of payment such as a "tap and go" mobile-pay system or a credit or debit card more often than they see money given in exchange for a receipt. They will see only electronic options for online shopping. Children who have grown up seeing mostly these payment methods may not be fully aware that actual money is involved.

This unit helps students understand that price is one of many things to consider when choosing between product options. The math skills used in this unit include addition, subtraction, multiplication, division, and using currency.

 Pacing/Lesson Plan

1. Distribute a copy of Rock-Climbing Gear on pages 20 and 21 to each student. Decide if you will have students read it in small groups or as a whole class. Note that the bold words in the story are defined on page 22.

2. Use the Discussion Questions on page 19 to lead a discussion with the class after reading Rock-Climbing Gear.

3. Distribute a copy of Store Vocabulary on page 22 to each student. Introduce the vocabulary words, rephrasing or explaining as needed. Then have students complete the activity.

4. Distribute a copy of Shopping Riddles on page 23 to each student. Provide support as needed as students complete the activity.

5. Distribute a copy of What Matters to You? on page 24 to each student. Provide support as needed as students complete the activity.

6. Distribute a copy of What Would You Buy? on page 25 to each student. Provide support as needed as students complete the activity.

7. Distribute a copy of At the Feed Store on page 26 to each student. Make play money or counters available for students. Provide support as needed as students complete the activity.

8. Distribute a copy of Receipts on page 27 to each student. Make play money or counters available for students. Provide support as needed as students complete the activity.

9. Have students do the Shopping Role-Play activity on page 28. To prepare, make copies of Scenes and Roles on page 29 for each group. Gather the other needed materials.

Discussion Questions

Use these questions to lead a discussion with the class after reading the story. Feel free to rephrase these or add your own questions.

- Why were Adira and her dad at the store? *[to buy rock-climbing gear for Adira]*

- Why did Adira want the blue shoes? *[They looked cool; the woman on the poster was wearing them.]* Why did she choose the gray shoes? *[They were less expensive.]*

- Why did Adira buy the nicer chalk bag? *[It was on sale.]*

- What types of things do you think about when you buy something? Do you think only about how much money it costs, or do you think about other things?

- Have you ever spent money and then wished that you hadn't? Tell what happened.

 Materials

For word problems on pages 26 and 27:
- play money (see page 10)
- counters (optional)

For Shopping Role-Play on pages 28 and 29—each group of 3 or 4 students needs:
- Scenes and Roles, page 29
- a pencil

 Vocabulary Words

compare	consumer	debit card	discount
products	purchase	receipt	

Name _____

Rock-Climbing Gear

Adira and her dad were at an outdoor-gear store. Camping supplies and other **products** filled the entire place. Adira needed rock-climbing gear. Her dad was going to **purchase** climbing shoes, a harness, and a chalk bag for her.

Adira's eyes went straight to a really nice pair of blue shoes. A large poster nearby showed a woman climbing a steep cliff. She was wearing the same blue shoes. "Awesome!" Adira thought. She imagined herself climbing that cliff, gripping the rock hundreds of feet off the ground.

Her dad pulled a box off the shelf. "Try these gray shoes on," he said. "The sign says they are the best-selling shoe."

Adira looked at the shoes and frowned. "They're plain and boring," she said. "I don't want to buy something just because everyone else did. How about these blue ones?"

"Those cost a bit more, but try on both pairs and **compare** how they fit," Dad said. "That's more important. If they're too loose, you could get hurt."

"And if they're too tight, I could get blisters!" Adira tried on the climbing shoes. Both pairs felt tight, but they didn't rub against her heel or toes.

"They both feel fine," she admitted, "but the blue ones look so cool. Now I don't know which ones to buy."

Dad laughed. "This difficult choice is common for **consumers**. They ask themselves, 'Should I pay an extra $20 just to look cool, or should I save that $20 to spend on something else?'"

Adira looked at the popular gray shoes. She didn't like how they looked. But they did fit well, which was the most important thing. In fact, the gray shoes felt like they were made just for her feet. She sighed. "I guess I'll get the gray ones."

Buying at the Store

Next, Adira looked at the chalk bags. It's important to use chalk on your hands while climbing so your hands don't slip off the rocks. The bag just had to be sturdy and light, and all the bags were. She was looking at the prices when she spotted a bag with a cool bear logo on it. The bag had a "sale" sticker on it. With the **discount**, it cost less than all the rest. Adira pumped her fist. "Yes!"

Finally, they looked at harnesses. Her dad picked one out.

"Wait," Adira said. "I see one that costs a lot less money."

But, to Adira's surprise, Dad wasn't interested in cost. "The harness keeps you safe," he said. "I'm happy to spend extra money for the safest one!"

Dad and Adira went to the front of the store. A store clerk rang up everything. Dad paid with his **debit card**, and the clerk gave him a **receipt**.

"Thanks, Dad," Adira said. "I'm ready to go home now."

Dad shook his head. "I have a better idea. With the money we saved, you can get an extra session at the climbing gym."

Adira jumped for joy and hugged her dad. "Yes! Let's see how well all this new gear works!"

Store Vocabulary

1. Read the word or term. Read the definition.
2. Find the word or term in Rock-Climbing Gear and read the sentence.
3. Then write your own sentence below using the word or term.

compare   to look at how two or more things are different and alike

_____

consumer   a person who buys goods and services

_____

debit card   a card used to pay for things with money from a bank account

_____

discount   a price that has been lowered for a product or service

_____

product   something that is made and then sold

_____

purchase   to buy something

_____

receipt   a paper that shows what you bought and how much you paid

_____

Financial Literacy Lessons and Activities • EMC 3124 • © Evan-Moor Corporation

Shopping Riddles

Read the riddle. Write the vocabulary word or term that answers the question: **Which word or term am I?**

Word Box

compare	consumer	debit card	discount
products	purchase	receipt	

1. This can be a surprise that is nice:
a couple of dollars taken off the price.   _____

2. You found what you want; but wait, there's more!
You must do this before leaving the store.   _____

3. These can be all sorts of things,
like books or food or toys or gold rings.   _____

4. If you've ever bought scissors, paper, or glue,
if you've ever bought something, then this is you!   _____

5. This is a record of a shopping event:
the items you got and the money you spent.   _____

6. Too many choices can make your eyes pop,
so take time to do this when you go out and shop.   _____

7. When you're shopping for things and use this to pay,
money comes out of your account right away.   _____

Name _____

What Matters to You?

Consumers have many different reasons for buying certain products. We can look at many things. We look at the price. We think about ads we've seen for a product. We might think about how popular a product is. We also look at features such as the taste of a food, the fit of clothing, the colors of flowers, or the fun of a puzzle.

Circle the reasons that would make you want to buy something. Draw a line through the reasons that would **not** make you want to buy something. There are no right or wrong answers.

Your favorite celebrity uses it.	It's a product that your parents like.

If you buy one, you get another one for free.

A famous athlete uses it.	All your friends have bought it.

It costs less money than a similar product.

You've used other products from the same company.

It's the most popular type of a product.	It's on sale for half price.

It looks like it is fun to use or play with.

It has funny commercials on TV.	It's a product that makes you feel good.

Financial Literacy Lessons and Activities • EMC 3124 • © Evan-Moor Corporation

What Would You Buy?

Read the text and answer the questions. There are no right or wrong answers.

1. You are shopping for a pair of earbuds. You see the same earbuds that all your friends have. You see another pair of earbuds that cost less. You could download five more songs with the money that you would save. Which earbuds would you buy? Explain your choice.

_____

_____

_____

2. You go to the store to buy a pack of trading cards. You see a sign that says "Buy 2, Get 1 Free." Do you still buy one pack, or do you buy two packs so that you can get a third one for free? Explain your choice.

_____

_____

_____

3. Someone gave you $20 in cash as a gift. You want to buy a special toy with the money. But you find out that the toy costs more than $20. Do you use some of your own money to buy the toy? Or do you buy something else that costs less than $20? Explain your choice.

_____

_____

_____

Name _____

At the Feed Store

Joy raises chickens. Chickens eat scratch, which is a mix of seeds and grains. Joy buys large bags of scratch at a feed store. Read each word problem. Write your answers in the table.

1. Joy buys three 50-pound bags of scratch each month. One bag costs $18. How much does she spend in one month?

2. The feed store started selling 25-pound bags of scratch for $11.00 a bag. Joy would rather buy the 25-pound bags because they are easier to pick up. How many 25-pound bags would she need to buy to have the same amount of scratch as three 50-pound bags? How much would they cost?

3. The chickens lay eggs most of the year. Joy collects them every day. She usually collects 180 eggs each month. She puts them in egg cartons that hold 12 eggs. How many egg cartons does she fill in a month? Joy sells the eggs to her neighbors for $4 a carton. How much money does she make in a month?

What was bought or sold in a month	How many	Cost for one	Cost for a month
50-pound bags of scratch	3	$18	
25-pound bags of scratch		$11	
cartons of eggs filled and sold		$4	

Use the table to answer these questions.

4. If Joy keeps buying 50-pound bags of scratch, will she pay more for feed than she makes selling eggs?   **yes   no**

If Joy starts buying 25-pound bags of scratch, will she pay more for feed than she makes selling eggs?   **yes   no**

Buying at the Store

Name _____

Receipts

A receipt is a slip of paper that shows all the details about a purchase. Look at the receipt. Read the descriptions.

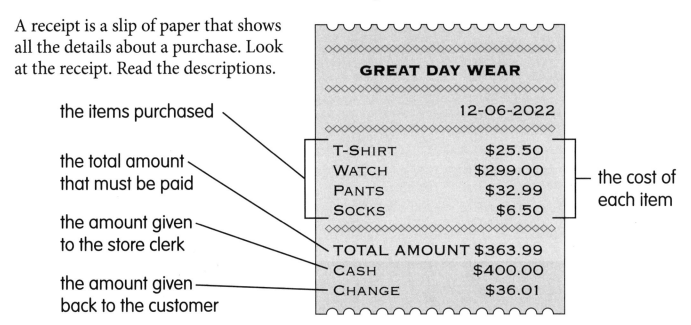

the items purchased

the total amount that must be paid

the amount given to the store clerk

the amount given back to the customer

GREAT DAY WEAR

12-06-2022

T-SHIRT	$25.50
WATCH	$299.00
PANTS	$32.99
SOCKS	$6.50

the cost of each item

TOTAL AMOUNT	$363.99
CASH	$400.00
CHANGE	$36.01

Look at each receipt. Write the missing numbers.

1.

The Book Branch	4/10/22
A Winter Den	$12.85
Butterfly bookmark	$0.99
Total	$_____
Cash	$15.00
Change	$_____

2.

Centerfield	12/5/22
Activity tracker	$65.80
Basketball	$22.49
Total	$_____
Cash	$_____
Change	$1.71

3.

Clothing Town	8/7/22
Jacket	$59.88
Shirt	$_____
Total	$83.10
Cash	$90.00
Change	$_____

4.

The STEM Store	10/11/22
Robot kit	$_____
STEM Activity Bk	$16.50
Total	$48.64
Cash	$_____
Change	$11.40

Buying at the Store

Name _____

Shopping Role-Play

Work in a small group in this role-play activity.

> ## WHAT YOU NEED
> - Scenes and Roles, page 29
> - a pencil

WHAT YOU DO

1. Get into groups of 3 or 4 students. Read each scene.

2. Decide which scene to use for your role-play. Decide who will be a customer and who will be a store clerk. You can have more than one of each.

3. If you are a **customer**, think about how you will make your decision:
   - Will you look at the item that you want to buy and try it out?
   - What features will you look at?
   - Will you ask the store clerk for his or her opinion?
   - Do you want to spend as little money as possible, or can you spend all of it?

   If you are a **store clerk**, think about what you will tell the customer:
   - Will you answer questions that the customer asks?
   - Will you try to get the customer to spend more money or get a good deal?
   - Will you tell your opinion of the items or say what other customers have said about them?

4. At the bottom of the Scenes and Roles sheet, write the scene you chose and who will play each role.

5. When you are ready, act out your role-play in front of the class. It can end any way you want: you can buy any item or choose not to buy one.

    Financial Literacy Lessons and Activities • EMC 3124 • © Evan-Moor Corporation

Buying at the Store

Name _____   Name _____

Name _____   Name _____

Scenes and Roles

SCENE 1: Sporting Goods Store

You go to a sporting goods store to buy a new soccer ball. They sell three different types. Your grandparents gave you $30. You also have $25 of your own money.

Play Like a Pro!

FIFA soccer ball $40

What Everyone Is Kicking!

HEXONIC

$35

Buy a ball now and save $15 on shin guards!

Budget Soccer Ball $30

SCENE 2: Bookstore

You go to a bookstore because you want to start reading a book series that the librarian told you about. You have no idea if you'll actually like the series. The series has three books. You've saved up $30 from your allowance.

The Long Trail

Book 1: Along the River

hardback $18

paperback $12

The Long Trail

3-book boxed set

hardcover $28

We chose Scene _____

Customer: _____

Store Clerk: _____

Earning Money at a Job

Understanding the Student Perspective

Children might not have regular jobs, but they often earn money doing chores around the house. Or they might work for a neighbor or family friend. While adults have jobs to pay for things they need, such as food, clothing, housing, and utilities, children usually earn money to buy things they want.

Children may be aware that people make different amounts of money. They may not realize that the amount of money is based on the skills and experience needed to do the job, as well as the effort required. Some jobs require special training, education, and skills.

This unit helps students understand what is involved when a person has a job. The math skills used in this unit include addition, subtraction, multiplication, division, and using graphs and currency.

Pacing/Lesson Plan

1. Distribute a copy of Back to School on pages 32 and 33 to each student. Decide if you will have students read it in small groups or as a whole class. Note that the bold words in the story are defined on page 34.

2. Use the Discussion Questions on page 31 to lead a discussion with the class after reading Back to School.

3. Distribute a copy of Job Vocabulary on page 34 to each student. Introduce the vocabulary words, rephrasing or explaining as needed. Then have students complete the activity.

4. Distribute a copy of Rocket Sneaks on page 35 to each student. Provide support as needed as students complete the activity.

5. Distribute a copy of Help Wanted on page 36 to each student. Provide support as needed as students complete the activity.

6. Distribute a copy of Job Application on page 37 to each student. Provide support as needed as students complete the activity.

7. Distribute a copy of Mother's Helper on page 38 to each student. Make play money or counters available for students. Provide support as needed as students complete the activity.

8. Distribute a copy of A Big Choice on page 39 to each student. Make play money or counters available for students. Provide support as needed as students complete the activity.

9. Have students play The Working Game on page 40. To prepare, make copies of the Game Board on page 41 for each group. Gather the other needed materials.

Discussion Questions

Use these questions to lead a discussion with the class after reading the story. Feel free to rephrase these or add your own questions.

- Why was Lupita surprised that her mom was going to college? *[Her mom already had a job.]*

- Why was her mom taking classes? *[so she can do more things at work]*

- What responsibilities do you have?

- Why do you think it could be good to have responsibilities at work?
  Why do you think it might not be good to have responsibilities at work?

- What kind of job will you want to have someday? Would you be willing to go to school to learn to do this job?

 Materials

For word problems on pages 38 and 39:
- play money (see page 10)
- counters (optional)

For The Working Game on pages 40 and 41—each group of 3 or 4 students needs:
- Game Board, page 41
- $3,000 in play money (see page 10)
- a die
- distinct game pieces (beads, coins, buttons, or other small objects)

 Vocabulary Words

benefit	business	entrepreneur
raise	responsibility	salary

Back to School

After dinner, Lupita helped her mom clean up. Then she opened her laptop to work on a school assignment. She was making a slideshow about kangaroos. Her mom sat down next to her and opened her own laptop.

"Do you have schoolwork, too?" Lupita asked, joking.

To her surprise, Mom said, "Yes, I'm going to college."

Lupita was confused. "What about your job? Are you going away to college? What about me?"

Mom laughed. "No, Lupita. I'm taking classes online. And I'm taking them *because* of my job."

"But why would you go to school if you already have a job?" Lupita asked. Her mom worked in an office. Her boss was an **entrepreneur** who owned several food trucks. Why did Mom need to take classes?

"Right now, I do a lot of simple tasks," Mom said, "like answering the phone. My boss is paying for me to go to school so I can learn more about the **business**. College is a **benefit** that I get with my job. Then my boss will give me more **responsibility** at work."

Lupita and her mom sat quietly for a little while. Lupita tried to do her work, but she was still confused.

"That doesn't make sense to me," she said. "You have to go to school. Then your boss will make you work harder?"

Mom looked up from her laptop and smiled. "Yes," she said. "But it's a good thing, not a bad thing. After this, I'll be able to do more at work. I'll have a whole new set of useful skills. And my boss will be able to give me a **raise**. My **salary** will be much higher."

"Oh, wow," Lupita said. "That's exciting! We'll be rich!"

"Well, we won't be rich," Mom said. "But it'll be nice to earn more money." Mom returned to her work. Lupita looked on the Internet for a kangaroo photo.

Name _____

"I've got an idea!" Mom said suddenly. "Why don't you come to work with me one day? I can show you what I do now and what I hope to do after my college classes."

Lupita bit her lip. "Well, I already know what answering the phone looks like, and shouldn't I be in school every day?"

"You don't have school next Monday," Mom reminded her. "It's a holiday for you, but food never takes a holiday."

"Oh, okay," Lupita said. "I guess I'll hang out with you at work."

When they arrived at Mom's small office Monday morning, she showed Lupita around and introduced her to the small crew. "Everyone, this is my daughter, Lupita. Lupita, this is Sylvia. She handles our budget. And this is Ben. He handles our social media sites. And over there is Fumi, who makes our fliers and ads."

"Wow," Lupita's eyes lit up. "I had no idea that there were so many different types of jobs with a food truck business! Can I watch you?"

Sylvia, Ben, and Fumi took turns showing Lupita what they do. At lunch, Mom asked Lupita what she thought. "I want to do what Fumi does when I grow up!" Lupita said. "I never thought you could do art for a business. She showed me some fliers that she made. She also let me draw in her sketchbook." Lupita held a page in front of her mother. "Fumi asked me to draw a design for a food festival flier that she needs for next month. Look at what I did!"

"Oh!" Mom said. "That's very creative!"

"Now I understand why you would take classes to learn new things!" Lupita said. "Do you think they have art classes in college?"

Name _____

Job Vocabulary

1. Read the word. Read the definition.
2. Find the word in Back to School and read the sentence.
3. Then write your own sentence below using the word.

benefit   something that is helpful

_____

business   an activity that is used to make money

_____

entrepreneur   a person who starts his or her own business

_____

raise   an increase in how much money a worker is paid

_____

responsibility   a duty or a task that someone is supposed to do

_____

salary   the money that a worker is paid

_____

Financial Literacy Lessons and Activities • EMC 3124 • © Evan-Moor Corporation

Rocket Sneaks

Read the story. Write the vocabulary word from the word box to complete each sentence. Then read the story again.

Word Box

benefit	business	entrepreneur
raise	responsibility	salary

When I grow up, I don't want to have a regular job. Instead, I want to be an

_____ and start my own company called Rocket Sneaks.

We'll make sneakers with small rockets attached. I don't know how they'll work

yet. I still have to invent them. But once I do, I'm sure they'll be popular. I'll be very

busy running my _____, of course. I'll probably hire my

little brother to help. His main _____ will be testing the

sneakers to see if they're safe. I plan to pay him a _____

of $5,000 a year. If he doesn't break anything or make a mess, I will give him

a _____ the next year. Plus, he'll get to fly around

in rocket sneakers. How many jobs come with

a _____ like that?

Name _____

Help Wanted

Read the story and the job descriptions. Then answer the items. There are no right or wrong answers.

When Mara turned 14, she wanted to buy a $600 mountain bike. Her parents said they'll pay for most of it, but Mara needs to pay $100 of it. To do that, Mara plans to get a part-time job. She found two possible jobs.

JOB #1

Help Wanted

I'm looking for someone to help on a farm. Responsibilities include feeding animals, cleaning stalls, and collecting eggs. Salary is $12 an hour, five hours a week.

JOB #2

Help Wanted

I need someone to work in my bakery. Responsibilities include cleaning out the mixer, sweeping the floor, and wiping down tables. Salary is $8 an hour, two hours after school, three days a week. Employees also get a free cookie.

If you were Mara, which job would you take? _____

Explain your choice. _____

_____

_____

_____

Name _____

Job Application

When you apply for a job, you may be asked to fill out a job application. This is a form that asks questions about you. The application might have questions that ask your age, what kinds of work you have done, and why you want the job.

> Think of a store or other place where you would like to work. Now imagine that you're applying for a job there. Complete the application. There are no right or wrong answers.

Name: _____ Age: _____

Job you are applying for: _____

List any skills or talents that you have. _____ _____

_____ _____ _____

_____ _____ _____

Have you done this kind of work before? _____ If so, tell us what you did.

_____

_____

Why do you want this job? _____

_____

_____

_____

_____

Name _____

Mother's Helper

Read each word problem. Write your answers.

1. Tiana's neighbor hired her to be a mother's helper. Tiana helps care for her neighbor's sons. Tiana earns $9.00 an hour. She works 3 hours on Saturdays and 4 hours on Sundays. How much money does Tiana earn each week?

   $_____

2. One day, Tiana had to work an extra half hour. How much extra did she earn for working later on that day? $_____

3. Tiana found out that if she takes a first-aid class, she can earn more money. The class costs $22.00.

   How many hours will Tiana need to work to earn that much?   _____

   After paying for the class, how much money will Tiana have left that week? $_____

4. Tiana is now trained in first aid. Her neighbor gave her a raise of $1.50 an hour. How much does she earn for working one hour now? $_____

A Big Choice

Jayce wants to get a summer job so he can buy a pair of wireless earbuds. They cost $149. Read the job descriptions. Use them to do the items.

Art Studio Assistant
Time: work 2 hours a day, 4 days a week   Salary: $8.00 an hour
Responsibilities: helping young children, organizing art supplies, cleaning up

Gardener
Time: work 2 hours a day, twice a week   Salary: $9.00 an hour
Responsibilities: digging, planting, and weeding in my garden

Animal Rescue Helper
Time: 4 hours a day, 3 times a week   Salary: $7.00 an hour
Responsibilities: walking, feeding, and playing with dogs

1. Complete the table. Figure out the weekly salary for each job.

	Hours a week	Hourly salary	Weekly salary
Art Studio Assistant			
Gardener			
Animal Rescue Helper			

2. Complete the graph to show how many weeks it would take Jayce to save $149.

Art Studio Assistant								
Gardener								
Animal Rescue Helper								
	1	2	3	4	5	6	7	8

3. If you were Jayce, which job would you take? _____

Explain why. _____

The Working Game

In this game, players earn money working at a company. All players earn $10 an hour. All players usually work 12 hours each week. But some weeks aren't usual! A roll of the die decides how much they will earn each week.

SETUP

- Get into groups of 3 or 4 players. Choose one player to be the banker.
- Gather materials: 1 die, game pieces, Game Board on page 41, play money (page 10)

PLAY

The object of the game is to earn the most money by the end of the game.

Place the game pieces on Week 1 of the Game Board.

The first player rolls the die.

- Find the number that was rolled in the "What Happened?" part of the board.

- Read the words next to the number you rolled.
- Use the Pay Rates below or on the Game Board to figure out what you earn for the week.

- Get your income from the banker.
- Move your game piece to the next week.

Repeat for each player for all 12 weeks.

The player who has earned the most money at the end of Week 12 wins.

Pay Rates
Pay rate for an hour: $10
Pay rate for a day: $40
Pay rate for a week: $120

Game Board

Week 1	**What Happened?**
Week 2	⚀ You are out sick. You lose one day of pay.
Week 3	⚁ You got a raise! Starting on your next turn, get $5 extra every week.
Week 4	⚂ You were late to work. Lose one hour of pay.
Week 5	⚃ There are no changes to your hours or salary this week.
Week 6	⚄ You earned a benefit: 1 day of paid time off. The next time you roll a 1, you still get paid.
Week 7	⚅ You can spend $25 to take a class. If you do, you get a raise. Starting on your next turn, get $10 extra every week.
Week 8	
Week 9	
Week 10	**Pay rate for an hour: $10**
Week 11	**Pay rate for a day: $40**
Week 12	**Pay rate for a week: $120**

Making and Following a Budget

Understanding the Student Perspective

Some children may think that people spend money any time they want, as long as they have some. They may not realize that adults might go shopping for a specific thing or with a dollar limit in mind. When people set up a budget for themselves, they figure out a plan for using their money. Based on a person's earnings, a budget shows how much money to reserve for necessary expenses such as food, housing, and bills; how much the person wants to save; and how much is available to spend on other things. A budget may sound like something that restricts the spending of money, but it actually allows us to make sure that our needs are met. A budget can help people figure out how important different buying choices are.

This unit helps students understand how a budget works and how planning can help reach a goal. The math skills used in this unit include addition, subtraction, multiplication, division, fractions, and using currency.

Pacing/Lesson Plan

1. Distribute a copy of A New BMX Bike on pages 44 and 45 to each student. Decide if you will have students read it in small groups or have two students read it aloud to the class. Note that the bold words in the dialogue are defined on page 46.

2. Use the Discussion Questions on page 43 to lead a discussion with the class after reading A New BMX Bike.

3. Distribute a copy of Budget Vocabulary on page 46 to each student. Introduce the vocabulary words, rephrasing or explaining as needed. Then have students complete the activity.

4. Distribute a copy of Budget Crossword Puzzle on page 47 to each student. Provide support as needed as students complete the activity.

5. Distribute a copy of How Important Is This? on page 48 to each student. Provide support as needed as students complete the activity.

6. Distribute a copy of If I Had a Hundred on page 49 to each student. Provide support as needed as students complete the activity.

7. Distribute a copy of Minh's Budget on page 50 to each student. Make play money or counters available for students. Provide support as needed as students complete the activity.

8. Distribute a copy of How Gabriela Uses Money on page 51 to each student. Make play money or counters available for students. Provide support as needed as students complete the activity.

9. Have students do the Create a Budget activity on page 52. To prepare, make copies of the Priority Cards on page 53 for each group. Gather the other needed materials.

Discussion Questions

Use these questions to lead a discussion with the class after reading the dialogue. Feel free to rephrase these or add your own questions.

- Why does Mei want a BMX bike? *[She wants a bike that she can use to do tricks.]*

- Finn said the new lamp was a want, not a need. What did he mean? *[It was just something Mei wanted to buy; her old lamp still works, so she doesn't need a new one.]*

- Do you like to plan how to use your money? Are you more like Finn or Mei?

- Have you ever set up a budget for yourself? Have you ever saved up money to buy something expensive?

 Materials

For word problems on pages 50 and 51:
- play money (see page 10)
- counters (optional)

For Create a Budget on pages 52 and 53—each group of 3 students needs:
- Priority Cards, page 53
- scissors
- a pencil

 Vocabulary Words

afford	budget	goal	manage
need	prioritize	want	

Name _____

A New BMX Bike

| **Characters** | Mei | a friend of Finn's who wants a new BMX bike |
| | Finn | Mei's friend |

Finn   Mei! Check out my new bike!

Mei   Awesome, Finn! I wish I could get a BMX bike. My bike is okay, but I can't do tricks with it. If I want a new one, my parents said I have to pay for it myself.

Finn   Do you have enough money?

Mei   I have some money in my savings account. But I need another $200 to **afford** a new BMX bike.

Finn   You can save up another $200, no problem!

Mei   No problem? Really? It's hard to save money. And it takes forever!

Finn   It could take a little while, but not forever. But I agree that it's not easy. How much do you get for your allowance?

Mei   My parents pay me $10 a week to do chores. Plus, I earn another $20 every Saturday as a mother's helper for Mrs. Guzman.

Finn   So you get $30 a week. That's great!

Mei   It is great! I always have enough money for gum and other things I want to buy.

   Financial Literacy Lessons and Activities • EMC 3124 • © Evan-Moor Corporation

Making and Following a Budget

Finn If you set up a **budget**, it will help you **manage** your money. If you save $25 each week, you'll have $200 in eight weeks.

Mei Hmm. I'll only have $5 a week to spend, though. I need to buy a new lamp this weekend, and it costs $18.

Finn Is your old lamp broken?

Mei No, I just don't like it anymore.

Finn So, you don't need to buy a new lamp—you just want to. When you're saving money, you have to **prioritize** what's more important and what's less important. Important things, like **needs**, are okay to spend money on. But **wants**…

Mei Let me guess. The new lamp is a want, since I don't need it.

Finn Right! So, what is more important: getting a new lamp right now or getting a new BMX bike in eight weeks?

Mei Well, if you put it that way, I guess it's the bike.

Finn Okay! Keep aiming for your **goal**, Mei: a new BMX bike!

Mei I will. And in eight weeks, we'll be able to practice bike tricks together!

Budget Vocabulary

1. Read the word. Read the definition.
2. Find the word in A New BMX Bike and read the sentence.
3. Then write your own sentence below using the word.

afford   to have enough money to buy something

_____

budget   a plan for how to use the money someone is earning

_____

goal   something a person is trying to do

_____

manage   to handle something in a successful way

_____

need   something that a person must have

_____

prioritize   to figure out what is important and what is not

_____

want   something that a person would like to have

_____

Name _____

Budget Crossword Puzzle

Find the vocabulary word that completes the sentence. Then write it in the crossword.

Word Box

afford   budget   goal   manage   needs   prioritize   wants

Across

4. My biggest _____ are boba tea, pizza, and a bracelet that I saw at the mall.

5. Make sure you save enough money for any _____ you might have.

7. After spending all his money on candy, Ajit decided to _____ which things are truly important.

Down

1. My new _____ lets me spend some money and save some more.

2. Ms. Brown came up with a plan to help her _____ her money.

3. My cousin wishes he could _____ a bluetooth speaker.

6. Her _____ right now is to save enough money for piano lessons.

How Important Is This?

When you prioritize, you organize things based on how important they are. You do this when you make a budget for yourself. Do the items below. There are no right or wrong answers.

1. Below are five things you might spend money on. Prioritize them in the table.
Write the most important thing next to **1** and the least important next to **5**.
Write the others next to **2**, **3**, or **4**.

a winter coat   a movie   toothpaste   a comic book   pizza with friends

1	
2	
3	
4	
5	

2. Think about six things that you have bought or that you have thought about buying.
Write each item in the basket that you think it belongs in.

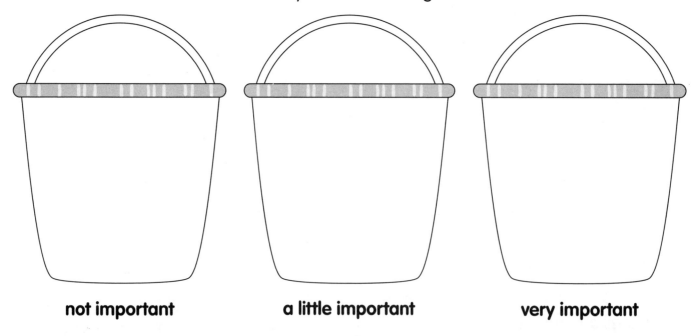

not important   **a little important**   **very important**

Name _____

If I Had a Hundred

Imagine that you just got a job. You earn $100 each week.
First, answer the questions. There are no right or wrong answers.

1. What do you like to spend money on? _____

_____

2. Name something you want to buy. _____

About how much does it cost? $_____

Now read the budgets below and answer the questions.

- Budget #1: Each week, put $100 into savings
- Budget #2: Each week, spend $20, put $80 into savings
- Budget #3: Each week, spend $50, put $50 into savings
- Budget #4: Each week, spend $80, put $20 into savings
- Budget #5: Each week, spend $30, put $50 into savings, donate $20

3. If you had to choose one budget, which one would it be? #_____
Explain why.

_____

_____

_____

4. Imagine that you need to save up for something that costs $200. How would you
change the budget you chose? Explain your new budget.

_____

_____

_____

Name _____

Minh's Budget

Minh made a budget when his dad started paying him to help at his family's restaurant. Read each word problem. Complete his budget using statements and clues in the word problems. Write each amount in the budget. Then answer the questions.

Minh's Weekly Budget

Earnings: $_____   Guitar lesson: $_____

Bank: $_____   Left over: $_____

Art class: $_____

---

1. Minh earns $45 each week by helping at his dad's restaurant. He puts 1/3 of what he earns in the bank. How much goes into the bank? $_____

How much is left over to spend now? $_____

2. Each week, Minh spends 1/5 of what is left over for his art class. His guitar lesson costs $4 more. How much money does he have left over after paying for both classes? $_____

3. Minh is saving money to buy a book for a friend. The book costs $26. How many weeks will it take him to save enough money for the book?   _____

VIETNAMESE CUISINE

Name _____

How Gabriela Uses Money

Gabriela earns a different amount of money each week. She always keeps $25 to spend. She puts the rest of her money into savings. Answer the questions.

Week	Earned	Spent	Saved
1	$65	$25	
2	$43	$25	
3	$72	$25	
4	$54	$25	
5	$67	$25	
6	$56	$25	

1. Complete the table. Figure out how much money Gabriela saved each week.

2. How much money did Gabriela earn in six weeks? $_____

3. How much money did Gabriela spend in six weeks? $_____

4. How much money did Gabriela save in six weeks? $_____

5. In Week 6, Gabriela spent $4.50 to go swimming and $12.25 to download songs. How much did she spend that day? $_____

6. Gabriela donated the rest of her spending money in Week 6 to the animal shelter. How much did she give to the shelter? $_____

Create a Budget

Work in a small group to plan a budget.

WHAT YOU NEED

- Priority Cards, page 53
- scissors
- a pencil

saving for a laptop
that costs $200

WHAT YOU DO

1. Get into groups of 3 students. Cut the Priority Cards apart. Spread them out so you can read them.

2. For each card, discuss whether it is a want or a need. Place them in separate piles. Then discuss how important each one is compared to the others. Put the cards in order from most important to least important.

3. Imagine that you each earn a salary of $100 each month. Discuss which items you can or cannot afford. Discuss these questions:

   - Will your salary allow you to pay for all your needs?
   - Will your salary allow you to pay for all your wants? If not, can you let some go?
   - Can you save some money to buy an item later?

4. Plan your own budget to show how you will use your salary each month.

Item	$ Amount

Financial Literacy Lessons and Activities • EMC 3124 • © Evan-Moor Corporation

Priority Cards

pizza on Friday nights:
$20 a month

prescription medicine:
$10 a month

streaming service showing your
favorite TV shows and movies:
$12 a month without ads
$6 a month with ads

paying back a loan:
$8 a month

saving for a bike
that costs $100

put money
into savings:
$5 a month

saving for a laptop
that costs $200

karate lessons:
$24 a month

groceries: $38 a month

bus fare to work: $18 a month

Using Banks

Understanding the Student Perspective

Children often save money that they received as a gift or from their allowance. Some children have difficulty keeping their money safe and organized. For cash, a small container works fine. But once children start receiving checks as gifts, it's time to open a bank account. Children may have seen their parents take out money from an ATM, but they may not realize that the money comes from the parents' account.

Children often see banks as a place where money is stored but not as a business. Banks store money so that they can lend it to people and businesses. Banks sometimes pay savers interest, as well as charging borrowers fees and interest for lending.

This unit helps students understand what banks do and how bank accounts work. The math skills used in this unit include addition, subtraction, multiplication, and using currency.

Pacing/Lesson Plan

1. Distribute a copy of An Interesting Visit to the Bank on pages 56 and 57 to each student. Decide if you will have students read it in small groups or as a whole class. Note that the bold words in the story are defined on page 58.

2. Use the Discussion Questions on page 55 to lead a discussion with the class after reading An Interesting Visit to the Bank.

3. Distribute a copy of Bank Vocabulary on page 58 to each student. Introduce the vocabulary words, rephrasing or explaining as needed. Then have students complete the activity.

4. Distribute a copy of All in a Day's Work on page 59 to each student. Provide support as needed as students complete the activity.

5. Distribute a copy of Savings Accounts on page 60 to each student. Provide support as needed as students complete the activity.

6. Distribute a copy of Checking Accounts on page 61 to each student. Provide support as needed as students complete the activity.

7. Distribute a copy of Riley's Bank Account on page 62 to each student. Make play money or counters available for students. Provide support as needed as students complete the activity.

8. Distribute a copy of Jayden's Bank Balance on page 63 to each student. Make play money or counters available for students. Provide support as needed as students complete the activity.

9. Have students play Earn Some, Spend Some, Owe Some on page 64. To prepare, make 2 copies of the Earn, Spend, and Owe Cards on page 65 for each group and cut them apart. Gather the other needed materials.

Discussion Questions

Use these questions to lead a discussion with the class after reading the story. Feel free to rephrase these or add your own questions.

- Why did Terrell's mom need to borrow money? *[She needed to replace her bakery's oven.]*

- The bank will lend Terrell's mom money. How will the bank make money doing that? *[It will charge her interest.]*

- Do you have a safe place to store your money? If so, where?

- Do you find it easy or difficult to keep track of your money?

- Do you think a bank account would be helpful for you? Why or why not?

 Materials

For word problems on pages 62 and 63:

- play money (see page 10)

- counters (optional)

For Earn Some, Spend Some, Owe Some on pages 64 and 65—each group of 4 students needs:

- 2 sets of Earn, Spend, and Owe Cards, page 65

- 4 balance sheets (see page 13)

- $100 in play money (see page 10)

- several dollars in coins

- 4 envelopes

- 4 pencils

 Vocabulary Words

account	ATM	balance	deposit
interest	minimum	teller	withdraw

Name _____

An Interesting Visit to the Bank

As the school bus drove away from his street, Terrell opened his mailbox. He grabbed a stack of envelopes and brought them inside. His mom was on the phone. She gave Terrell a quick wave as she talked. Terrell opened an envelope from his grandmother.

"Okay," Mom said to the person on the phone. "Yes, it needs to be fixed. I'll find a way. Thanks."

She hung up and sighed. The oven at her bakery had to be replaced. It was going to cost a lot of money.

"No problem," Terrell said. "Grandma sent me a $100 bill!" He placed the bill on the kitchen counter. Their cat, Fiona, pawed at it.

Mom laughed. "Thanks. But I need a lot more money than that. And you need to put that $100 somewhere safe before it becomes a cat toy. Let's go to the bank."

At the bank, Mom went to the counter to talk to a **teller**.

"I need to borrow some money," Mom said. "Also, I'd like to open an **account** for my son."

The teller called a banker. Soon, a woman invited Terrell and his mom into her office. First, they talked about a loan for Mom's bakery. Mom explained that she needed a new oven. She told the banker it would cost $8,000.

The banker typed on a keyboard and looked at the computer screen. "I see that you've taken out loans here before and paid them back on time," she said. "We can definitely lend you $8,000. The **interest** rate will be 5 percent."

"What does that mean?" Terrell asked.

"When a bank lends you money, it's providing a service," Mom explained. "The bank gets paid for that service by charging a small piece of the amount that you're borrowing."

Using Banks

"So they give you money, but you have to pay them for it?" asked Terrell.

"Yes, but I pay them a little at a time, along with the money I borrowed," Mom explained.

Mom filled out a bunch of papers. "We'll put the loan money in your checking account by Friday," the banker said. "You can **withdraw** it by writing a check or using the **ATM** any time after that."

Finally, it was time to set up Terrell's savings account. Mom filled out some more papers, and Terrell had to sign his name on the last page. Then the banker entered the information into the computer. "You need a **minimum** of $100 to open an account," the banker said.

"That's how much I brought!" Terrell replied, waving his $100 bill. He made his first **deposit**.

"You're starting with a **balance** of $100," the woman said. "But that amount will go up. You see, banks use money to make money. So, when you put money into a savings account, you're providing a service to that bank. You get paid for that service. The bank pays you…"

Terrell smiled. "Let me guess…interest?"

The banker laughed. "Yes!"

Name _____

Bank Vocabulary

1. Read the word. Read the definition.
2. Find the word in An Interesting Visit to the Bank and read the sentence.
3. Then write your own sentence below using the word.

account   an agreement where a bank keeps money for someone

_____

ATM   a bank machine that can take or give cash

_____

balance   the amount of money someone has in the bank

_____

deposit   money that is put into a bank account

_____

interest   money made by lending money or paid to borrow money

_____

minimum   the smallest amount

_____

teller   a person who works in a bank at the counter

_____

withdraw   to take out

_____

Name _____

All in a Day's Work

Read the story. Use the clue under each line to write a word to complete each sentence. You will write either a vocabulary word from the word box or a word that you think of.

Word Box

account   ATM   balance   deposited   interest   minimum   teller   withdraw

It was a busy day at the bank today. A customer wanted to borrow money to

open a _____ store. He has had an _____ with the
     adjective   vocabulary word

bank for _____ years, so we were happy to lend him the money.
     number

Then a new customer asked a _____ for help. She had just
                 vocabulary word

received her statement that showed every time she _____ money.
                        vocabulary word

She thought that the _____ was too high. I told her that her money
          vocabulary word

had earned some _____. She was really _____ when
          vocabulary word   emotion

she heard that!

The last customer of the day has a new job as a _____. He
                      job

held up his first paycheck and asked if it was more than the _____
                               vocabulary word

amount of money to open an account. It was! He was able to go to the

_____ and _____ $_____ from his
 vocabulary word   vocabulary word   number

new bank account!

Name _____

Savings Accounts

Read about the savings accounts. Then answer the questions. There are no right or wrong answers.

Savings accounts are for money that you don't plan to spend soon. Savings accounts usually earn interest. The higher your balance is, the more interest you earn. Sometimes accounts have monthly fees. For most accounts, you need to keep at least the minimum balance in your account. Some savings accounts do not let you use an ATM.

Savings Account #1
- 2¢ interest for every dollar in the account
- No minimum balance
- Can use the ATM

Savings Account #2
- 3¢ interest for every dollar in the account
- Can withdraw money 4 times each month
- Minimum balance of $500

Savings Account #3
- 4¢ interest for every dollar in the account
- $5 fee each month
- Minimum balance of $800

1. Which savings account would you choose? #_____ Explain why. _____

_____

_____

_____

2. What is something you might save for? _____

_____

_____

Name _____

Checking Accounts

Read about the checking accounts. Then answer the questions. There are no right or wrong answers.

Checking accounts are for money that you plan to spend. Banks have a minimum age, between 13 and 18, to open an account. When you open a checking account, you get checks and usually an ATM card. A checking account often has a monthly fee. Some banks won't charge the fee as long as you keep the minimum balance in the account.

Checking Account #1
- $1,000 minimum balance
- $10 fee if your balance goes below the minimum
- Can use the ATM

Checking Account #2
- $25 fee each month
- No minimum balance
- Can use the ATM

Checking Account #3
- $5 fee each month
- No minimum balance
- No ATM use

1. Which checking account would you choose? #_____ Explain why. _____

_____

_____

2. Do you think you would write checks or use the ATM more to buy things?

_____

Explain why.

_____

Name _____

Riley's Bank Account

Riley has a savings account at a bank. She keeps track of her balance. When she deposits money, the balance goes up. Her account earns interest. The interest also makes her balance go up. When she withdraws money to spend, the balance goes down.

Read each word problem. Write your answers.

1. Riley had $75.60 in her bank account. She withdrew $20 to buy a book. What was her new balance?

   $_____

2. Riley deposited one check for $43.25 and another for $17.50. How much did she deposit in all?

   $_____

3. Riley's bank balance is $116.10. She deposited a check for $25.05 and $19.00 in cash. What is her new balance?

   $_____

4. Riley has deposited more money. Her balance is now $190.00. Each month, her account earns interest. For each dollar, she earns 1¢.

   How much total interest will she earn this month?

   $_____

   What will her new balance be?

   $_____

 Financial Literacy Lessons and Activities • EMC 3124 • © Evan-Moor Corporation

Name _____

Jayden's Bank Balance

Jayden has a bank account. The table below shows one month of his account.

Read the action. Write the amount under **Deposit** or **Withdraw**. Then write the new balance under **Balance**. The first three lines are already completed.

Action	Deposit	Withdraw	Balance
Starting balance			$65.00
Put in $2.00	+ $2.00		$67.00
Take out $3.50		– $3.50	$63.50
Put in $11.75			
Put in $45.00			
Put in $7.10			
Take out $3.00			
Put in $8.50			
Put in $16.40			
Take out $12.25			
Put in $5.05			
Ending balance			

How much more money does Jayden have at the end of the month than he had at the beginning of the month?

$_____

Earn Some, Spend Some, Owe Some

In this game, money will go into and out of your bank account. Keep track of your money to win!

SETUP

- Gather materials: sets of 20 Earn, Spend, and Owe Cards (page 65); balance sheets (page 13); play money (page 10); several dollars in coins; envelopes, pencils

- Get into groups of 4 players. Choose one player to be the banker.

- Each player gets an envelope, a balance sheet, and a pencil. Each player writes his or her name on the envelope and balance sheet. Write **$20** at the top of the Balance column on the balance sheet. The envelope is the player's bank account.

- Each player gets $20 for his or her bank account. Place the rest of the money in front of the banker. Place the cards facedown in one pile.

PLAY

The object of the game is to keep track of how much money you earn and spend. Start with the player to the left of the banker. On each turn, a player takes a card and reads it aloud.

- If it is an **Earn** card, the banker gives all players either the payday amount or the interest on their current balance. They record the deposit on their balance sheet.

- If it is a **Spend** card, each player decides if he or she will spend the money. Players who spend: ○ pay the banker and then
  ○ record the withdrawal on their balance sheet.

- If it is an **Owe** card, each player looks at his or her current balance. If it is below $10, they pay a $3 fee to the banker.

- Players who run out of money cannot spend any more until they earn more money.

After all cards have been read, all players count the money in their bank account and compare it to the last balance on their balance sheet. All players with matching bank accounts and balance sheets win!

Earn, Spend, and Owe Cards

Buy a snack at school. **Spend** $3.

Download a new song. **Spend** $1.

Payday! Everyone **earns** $5.

Go to lunch with friends. **Spend** $6.

Buy the next book in your favorite series. **Spend** $7.

Payday! Everyone **earns** $5.

Buy gum. **Spend** $2.

Buy pizza at the mall. **Spend** $4.

Check your balance. If it is below $10, you **owe** $3.

Check your balance. For every dollar, you **earn** 4¢ in interest.

Raising Money to Help Others

 Understanding the Student Perspective

Children are often involved with fundraisers held at school. They may also belong to or be familiar with groups or teams that have raised money. They may have seen commercials on TV or notices online about fundraising efforts, and their parents may support some of them. However, they may not realize why these needs exist, especially those outside of their own communities. Charities can provide resources to people struggling with hardships, such as poverty, homelessness, food insecurity, disease, or natural disaster, or raising money for underfunded causes, such as wildlife sanctuaries, educational programs, scientific research, and the arts.

This unit helps students understand how and why people might raise money to help others. The math skills used in this unit include addition, subtraction, multiplication, and using currency.

 Pacing/Lesson Plan

1. Distribute a copy of WeHelp on pages 68 and 69 to each student. Decide if you will have students read it in small groups or have two students read it aloud to the class. Note that the bold words in the dialogue are defined on page 70.

2. Use the Discussion Questions on page 67 to lead a discussion with the class after reading WeHelp.

3. Distribute a copy of Helping Others Vocabulary on page 70 to each student. Introduce the vocabulary words, rephrasing or explaining as needed. Then have students complete the activity.

4. Distribute a copy of Raising Riddles on page 71 to each student. Provide support as needed as students complete the activity.

5. Distribute a copy of Would You Donate? on page 72 to each student. Provide support as needed as students complete the activity.

6. Distribute a copy of Let's Put the Fun in Fundraiser! on page 73 to each student. Provide support as needed as students complete the activity.

7. Distribute a copy of The Art Show on page 74 to each student. Make play money or counters available for students. Provide support as needed as students complete the activity.

8. Distribute a copy of Holiday Meals on page 75 to each student. Make play money or counters available for students. Provide support as needed as students complete the activity.

9. Have students do the Plan a Fundraiser activity on page 76. To prepare, make copies of the Graphic Organizer on page 77. Gather the other needed materials.

Discussion Questions

Use these questions to lead a discussion with the class after reading the dialogue. Feel free to rephrase these or add your own questions.

- What is WeHelp raising money for? *[people affected by forest fires]*

- How will WeHelp raise money? *[They're putting on a music festival. They want donations of food, clothing, and money.]*
  Why do you think they are holding an event instead of just asking for donations?

- What is Natalie going to do at the festival? Why is it important to her to help out? *[She's going to sell raffle tickets. She was once homeless and knows how great it is when others help out.]*

- Have you ever helped out with a cause? Did you help by giving money or in some other way? Tell about the cause and how you helped.
  (If needed, give examples of causes, such as homelessness; poverty; cure for cancer; caring for the environment; victims of flooding, fire, hurricane, tornado, or earthquake; stray animals; or any causes that affect your region.)

 Materials

For word problems on pages 74 and 75:
- play money (see page 10)
- counters (optional)

For Plan a Fundraiser on pages 76 and 77—each group of 3 students needs:
- Graphic Organizer, page 77
- poster board or a large sheet of paper
- colored markers
- a pencil

 Vocabulary Words

cause	charity	donate	food bank
fundraiser	homeless	organization	volunteer

Name _____

WeHelp

Characters	Natalie	a friend of Aviv
	Aviv	a friend of Natalie

Aviv   A bunch of us are going to play kickball on Saturday morning. Want to join us?

Natalie   That sounds fun, but I can't. I'm going to a **fundraiser** for WeHelp. The **organization** is raising money to help people who were affected by the forest fires.

Aviv   I heard about that. A lot of houses burned down, right?

Natalie   Yes. Luckily, nobody was hurt. But a lot of families are now **homeless**.

Aviv   That's terrible. What is WeHelp doing to help?

Natalie   They're hosting a small music festival. They're asking everyone who goes to **donate** money, food, or clothing. They're working with the **food bank** in Center City.

Aviv   I know that place! We collected canned goods for them in the fall. I brought in a whole bunch of tuna.

Natalie   *(Laughing)* I remember that! Anyway, the food bank is planning to provide lots of meals to families who lost their homes.

Raising Money to Help Others

Name _____

Aviv — So, what are you going to do at the fundraiser? Listen to music?

Natalie — I'll listen to some music. But the real reason I'm going is to be a **volunteer**. There's going to be a raffle, and I'm going to help sell raffle tickets. All the money from the tickets will be donated to the families.

Aviv — I can't imagine what it's like being homeless or needing to get food from the food bank. Can you?

Natalie — Actually, I can. Before I moved here last year, my family was homeless for a few months.

Aviv — I had no idea!

Natalie — Well, I haven't told too many people. It was scary. But it was also nice when people helped us. My mom didn't want to accept **charity**, but the donations we got helped us get back on our feet quickly. Now my mom and I try to "give back" whenever we can.

Aviv — Helping people who are homeless sounds like such a great **cause**! Forget about kickball. Can I come with you and help?

Natalie — You bet!

WeHelp
presents benefit concert for families who lost their homes to the wildfires.

Helping Others Vocabulary

1. Read the word or term. Read the definition.
2. Find the word or term in WeHelp and read the sentence.
3. Then write your own sentence below using the word or term.

cause   a reason for helping; a constant challenge

_____

charity   aid that is given to someone who is in need

_____

donate   to give something away for free

_____

food bank   a place that collects food for people who need it

_____

fundraiser   a way to collect money for something

_____

homeless   not having an indoor place to live

_____

organization   a group that works together to do something

_____

volunteer   a person who does a task without getting paid

_____

          Financial Literacy Lessons and Activities • EMC 3124 • © Evan-Moor Corporation

Raising Riddles

Read the riddle. Write the vocabulary word or term that answers the question.

Word Box

cause　　charity　　donate　　food bank
fundraiser　　homeless　　organization　　volunteer

FOOD BANK DONATION

1. Natural disaster? People to feed?
   An event like this helps those in need.　What it it? _____

2. She won't get paid, but she doesn't mind.
   She likes to help out, just to be kind.　Who is she? _____

3. Someone who is this might have said,
   "I wish I had a roof over my head."　What is it? _____

4. Got extra food? Outgrown your shoes?
   You can do this with things you don't use.　What can you do? _____

5. To help others—that is our dream. And
   working together, we make a great team.　What are we? _____

6. This place feeds people every day. The
   people who come in don't have to pay.　What is it? _____

7. If a fire or hurricane hits your street,
   this can help you get back on your feet.　What is it? _____

8. Whether you give a dollar or a dime,
   doing this to help is worth your time.　What is it? _____

Name _____

Would You Donate?

There are lots of opportunities to help others by donating money or goods. Several websites allow people to post what they are raising money for. They explain their situation and ask for donations.

Read each post. Circle whether you would donate to it. Then explain your choice. There are no right or wrong answers.

1. I am raising money to help people on a Caribbean Island. There was a huge hurricane, and many of them lost their homes. They need food, water, and shelter.   **yes**   **no**

Explain: _____

_____

_____

2. My rowing team needs a new boat. The one we have is old, and we'd like to have a new one before our next competition.   **yes**   **no**

Explain: _____

_____

_____

3. I'm raising money for my neighbor. His wife is very sick. He has to take care of her and their two children. He misses a lot of work because of this. Plus, the family now has lots of medical bills.   **yes**   **no**

Explain: _____

_____

_____

Name _____

Let's Put the Fun in Fundraiser!

Read about each organization. Read each type of fun fundraising event. Then draw a line from the organization to the fundraiser that you think will work best for it. An organization can have more than one fundraiser. There are no right or wrong answers.

ORGANIZATION

Sport Kids runs athletic clubs for kids who can't afford the cost of being on a team.

Doctors Care sends doctors to other countries after natural disasters such as hurricanes.

Land Friends sets up hiking trails for everyone to enjoy.

Little Sprouts runs a daycare center for families who can't find affordable child care.

We Are the Cure raises money for cancer research.

FUNDRAISER

• Art show

• Bake sale

• Fun run or walk

• Pizza party

• Bike-a-thon

• Ball contest

• Donated items sale

Name _____

The Art Show

Hyun's class wants to raise money for the local fire department. The class will host a fundraiser in the school cafeteria. It will be an art show. They'll provide snacks and drinks. They'll raise money by selling their artwork.

Read each word problem. Write your answers.

1. The class spent $13.50 on lemonade. They spent $32.75 on snacks. They also spent $10.50 on decorations. How much did it cost to put together the art show? $_____

2. Hyun sold three paintings in the show. One sold for $14.00. The second one sold for $17.50. The third one sold for $15.00. How much money did Hyun's paintings raise? $_____

3. By the end of the show, all the artwork had been sold. The class raised $674.00. A local business offered to match that donation. So now the class had another $674.00. How much money did they raise in all? $_____

Name _____

Holiday Meals

Bennett is helping collect money for his local food bank. The food bank needs to provide holiday meals for nine families. Use the table to do the items.

Food	Price	How many for one family?	Total cost for one family
turkey	$20.25	1	$20.50
can of green beans	$1.50	3	
bag of potatoes	$3.75	2	
can of cranberry sauce	$2.50	2	
bag of rolls	$6.00	1	
pie	$7.75	2	

1. Complete the table.

2. What is the total price of the meal for one family? $_____

3. What will it cost to provide meals for 9 families? $_____

4. The food bank has collected $184.00 so far. How much more do they need for all the holiday meals? $_____

Name _____

Plan a Fundraiser

You will work in a group to plan a small fundraiser. You can collect money, clothing, food, or anything else.

WHAT YOU NEED

- Graphic Organizer, page 77
- poster board or a large sheet of paper
- a pencil
- colored markers

WHAT YOU DO

1. Get into groups of 3 students. Choose someone to write your group's ideas on the Graphic Organizer.

2. Choose a cause that everyone in the group is interested in. Here are some ideas:
   - Collect food for a local food bank.
   - Raise money for a wildlife park.
   - Collect used clothing for a homeless shelter.
   - Raise money for something in your school.

3. Research your cause. Here are things to think about:
   - What is the problem? Why is it a problem?
   - What do you need to help solve it? If possible, contact the place you're trying to help or the organization that you will donate to and ask what they need the most. The answer might surprise you. An animal shelter might need paper towels, or a food bank might need only certain food items.

4. Decide if you will collect money or goods for a set time or if you will hold an event to raise money. If you hold an event, decide what type of event.

5. Make a poster to tell people how to donate or about your event. Use information from your Graphic Organizer. The poster should use both words and pictures to make people want to donate.

   Bonus: Hold the fundraiser that you planned. Donate what you collect to the cause you chose.

Graphic Organizer

Causes we are thinking about:

_____   _____

_____   _____

_____   _____

Our choice: _____

Who will be helped? _____

What should people donate?

money   food   clothes   toys   other _____

How will this help? _____

_____

How much or how many do you need? _____

How will you collect what you need? _____

When will you collect? We'll collect from _____ to _____
date   date

or at an event on _____.
date

Planning a Party

Understanding the Student Perspective

People often host parties to celebrate something. A party might be held to celebrate an important event or accomplishment, honor a person, celebrate a holiday, or enjoy a sporting event as a group. There are many occasions to celebrate and diverse ways to celebrate them. Most children have been to parties, but some may not yet understand the costs involved. Party planning involves a balance between creating a fun event while not spending more money than you can afford. The person planning the party must decide between a variety of options regarding food, theme, and decorations.

This unit helps students understand how a party is planned and paid for. The math skills used in this unit include addition, subtraction, multiplication, and using currency.

Pacing/Lesson Plan

1. Distribute a copy of The Volleyball Party on pages 80 and 81 to each student. Decide if you will have students read it in small groups or as a whole class. Note that the bold words in the story are defined on page 82.

2. Use the Discussion Questions on page 79 to lead a discussion with the class after reading The Volleyball Party.

3. Distribute a copy of Party-Planning Vocabulary on page 82 to each student. Introduce the vocabulary words, rephrasing or explaining as needed. Then have students complete the activity.

4. Distribute a copy of Party Riddles on page 83 to each student. Provide support as needed as students complete the activity.

5. Distribute a copy of The Fancy Gala on page 84 to each student. Provide support as needed as students complete the activity.

6. Distribute a copy of Make an Invitation on page 85 to each student. Provide support as needed as students complete the activity.

7. Distribute a copy of Hi, Neighbors! on page 86 to each student. Make play money or counters available for students. Provide support as needed as students complete the activity.

8. Distribute a copy of Which Costs More? on page 87 to each student. Make play money or counters available for students. Provide support as needed as students complete the activity.

9. Have students do the It's Party Time! activity on page 88. To prepare, make copies of The Party Store on page 89 for each group. Gather the other needed materials. If desired, display their invitation fliers and have students vote on which party they would most like to attend.

Discussion Questions

Use these questions to lead a discussion with the class after reading the story. Feel free to rephrase these or add your own questions.

- Who is coming to Ananda's party? Why are they having the party? *[the volleyball team; because they improved a lot]*

- Why didn't they order chicken from their favorite chicken place? *[It was going to cost too much.]*

- Have you gone to a party recently? Tell about it.
  Have you or your family hosted a party recently? Tell about it.

- What types of celebrations do you have in your home?

 Materials

For word problems on pages 86 and 87:
- play money (see page 10)
- counters (optional)

For It's Party Time! on pages 88 and 89—each group of 3 students needs:
- The Party Store, page 89
- $80 to $120 in play money (see page 10)
- a die
- two sheets of paper
- a pencil
- colored pencils, crayons, or markers

 Vocabulary Words

| celebration | favors | host |
| invitation | prefer | quantity |

Name _____

The Volleyball Party

"Good news, Dad!" Ananda said. "Jackie got her **invitation**. Her mom said she can come to the party."

"Great," Dad said. "So, the final guest total is 12."

Ananda and her dad were planning a party for Ananda's volleyball team. Dad was the coach. The team improved a lot during the season. Dad thought they should have a **celebration**.

"Let's get sushi," Ananda said. "It's my favorite food!"

"I love sushi, too," Dad said. "But I don't know if everyone on the team does. Besides, it might feel too fancy for a volleyball party."

"Chicken!" Ananda said. "And it has to be from Dominick's!"

"I **prefer** Dominick's, too," Dad said. "But there will be 12 guests, plus us. That requires a large **quantity** of chicken. I'll call around and get prices."

Ananda sighed. "I get it. When you're the **host** of a party, you have to think about how much stuff costs."

"Yes," Dad said. "We need to find a balance between what we do and the cost. We want the party to be lots of fun. But we need to stick to a budget."

Dad called Dominick's Chicken. "Hi," he said. "I'm hosting a party this Saturday. I'm wondering what it would cost to get chicken wings, salad, and lemonade for 14 people." Dad wrote something down. Then he called two other chicken places and wrote more notes.

Ananda looked at the paper. "Ugh," she said. "Dominick's will be so expensive!"

Of the other two chicken places, Ananda and Dad chose Elroy's. It cost a little more than the third one, Chuck's Charbroiler, but the chicken was much juicier. Dad called Elroy's back and placed the order for Saturday.

At the grocery store, Ananda and her dad bought some snacks. Then they went to a sporting goods store. Ananda wanted to get **favors** for all her friends. She thought about gifts she had gotten in the past.

"Jackie got me a soccer ball for my birthday," she thought. "Maybe I can get everyone a volleyball…." Then she saw the price for a volleyball. She gulped. "I can't buy 12 volleyballs!" Finally, Ananda found pretty, colorful wristbands that didn't cost much. "Perfect!" Ananda said.

Ananda looked at her backyard, where the party would be. It was pretty, but she wanted it to look festive. She was also hoping to have a party game. But there wasn't much money left in the budget.

As she stared at the volleyball net in her yard, she suddenly had an idea! She would buy some balloons and put one wristband inside each one. Then she would blow up the balloons and tie each one to the net. Her teammates could take turns throwing a ball at a balloon. When it popped, they would get their favor! "This will be a great party!" she thought.

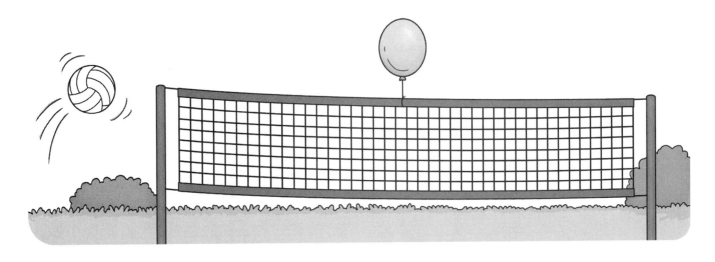

Name _____

Party-Planning Vocabulary

1. Read the word. Read the definition.
2. Find the word in The Volleyball Party and read the sentence.
3. Then write your own sentence below using the word.

celebration   a party that honors a person, place, thing, or idea

_____

favors   gifts that are given out at a party

_____

host   someone who has a party

_____

invitation   a note asking someone to come to a party

_____

prefer   to like one thing more than another

_____

quantity   an amount or a number

_____

     Financial Literacy Lessons and Activities • EMC 3124 • © Evan-Moor Corporation

Name _____

Party Riddles

Read the riddle. Write the vocabulary word that answers the question: **Which word am I?**

> **Word Box**
>
> celebration   favors   host
>
> invitation   prefer   quantity

1. Throwing a party? Send one of these.
It says to your friends, "You can come if you please." _____

2. It could be a few. It could be a lot.
This is the word for how many you've got. _____

3. When a party takes place, he or she is the one
who makes sure the guests have lots of fun. _____

4. Is today important? Did you win a big race?
Then maybe it's time one of these took place! _____

5. You do this when you shop at a store
and you pick out the option that you like more. _____

6. These are gifts that each guest receives.
They go home at the end, when everyone leaves. _____

Name _____

The Fancy Gala

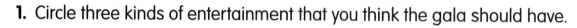

Art Foundation is planning a fancy party called a gala. This gala will help raise money for local art programs. Tickets cost $200 for each person.

Read about the plans below. Circle or write your choices. There are no right or wrong answers.

1. Circle three kinds of entertainment that you think the gala should have.

a magician	a pop music band	a clown	a lion tamer
a jazz band	a photography show	a juggler	a comedian

2. Art Foundation is planning food for the gala. For the first hour, 3 different snacks will be served. Then everyone will sit down for a nice dinner. Guests can choose from 3 different dinner choices. Finally, dessert will be served. Write your ideas for all the foods that guests will have at the gala.

Snacks:

1. _____

2. _____

3. _____

Dinner:

1. _____

2. _____

3. _____

Dessert:

1. _____

Financial Literacy Lessons and Activities • EMC 3124 • © Evan-Moor Corporation

Name _____

Make an Invitation

Art Foundation's gala is all planned. Now it's time to send out invitations. In the space below, make an invitation for the gala. You can add any date and time that you like. Draw a design that will make people want to go to the gala. Look at the sample invitations for ideas.

Planning a Party Name _____

Hi, Neighbors!

Faizel and his family just moved to a new town. They are having a "housewarming party" to meet their new neighbors. Read each word problem. Write your answers.

1. Faizel and his mom went to the party store to buy decorations. They bought paper plates for $6.50, balloons for $23.75, and streamers for $11.25. How much did they spend?

    $_____

2. Faizel found out that there are 12 children coming to the party. He wants to give each child a copy of his favorite book. The book costs $3. How much will it cost to buy a book for every child?

    $_____

3. They will need to feed 30 people. If they bought pizza, it would cost $150.00. But if they bought pizza dough, sauce, cheese, and toppings from the store, guests could make their own, and Faizel's family would learn what their neighbors like. These ingredients would cost $45.00. How much would they save if guests make their own pizzas?

    $_____

4. Faizel's new house has a pool in the backyard. His dad is buying floaty toys for guests to use in the pool. They are on sale for $11.00 each. How much will it cost for 8 floaty toys?

    $_____

 Financial Literacy Lessons and Activities • EMC 3124 •

Name _____

Which Costs More?

Imagine that you are hosting a party for 10 people. You need to decide what to drink and eat and how to entertain party guests.

Read each pair of options. Figure out how much each option will cost. Remember that you need enough for 10 people. Then write **<** or **>** in the circle to show which option costs more.

Drinks

1. **Option 1:** 4 large bottles of lemonade for $3.25 each $_____

    Option 2: 10 individual bottles of lemonade for $1.50 each $_____

    Option 1 ◯ **Option 2**

Food

2. **Option 1:** $16.50 for each pizza; one pizza for 3 people $_____

    Option 2: $6 for each sushi roll; one roll for each person $_____

    Option 1 ◯ **Option 2**

Entertainment

3. **Option 1:** a magician; $250 an hour for 1 1/2 hours $_____

    Option 2: rock climbing at a climbing gym; $35 for each person $_____

    Option 1 ◯ **Option 2**

Name _____

It's Party Time!

You will work in a small group to plan an imaginary party for your entire class and figure out what it will cost.

WHAT YOU NEED

- The Party Store, page 89
- a die
- play money ($80 to $120 for each group)
- two sheets of paper
- a pencil
- colored pencils, crayons, or markers

WHAT YOU DO

1. Get into groups of 3 students.

2. Roll a die until you get either a **4**, **5**, or **6**. Multiply that number by 20. This is your budget, the total amount you can spend. Ask your teacher for your budget in play money.

3. Use The Party Store page to plan a menu. Decide as a group on a theme for the party. Then decide what drinks, snacks, food, dessert, and other items you will need for your party.

4. Write everything you will buy for your party, along with the price. Use your play money or paper and pencil to figure out how much everything costs and make sure it is within your budget. If your total cost is higher than your budget, make some changes to your choices. Then circle what you will buy on The Party Store.

5. Design an invitation flier for your party.

Planning a Party

Name _____

Name _____

Name _____

The Party Store

 Drinks:
- large lemonade (serves 4 people; $3.50)
- large iced tea (serves 4 people; $4.00)
- large fruit punch (serves 3 people; $2.75)
- bottle of water (serves 2 people; $2.00)

 Snacks:
- fruit or veggie platter ($11.50)
- box of crackers ($2.25)
- chips and dip ($8.50)
- bag of pretzels ($3.25)

 Food:
- pizza (serves 4 people; $12.00)
- sandwiches (one for each person; $3.25)

 **Dessert:**
- large cake (serves 20 people; $19.50)
- cookie plate (serves 10 people; $8.50)
- ice cream sundae bar including ice cream and toppings ($2.25 for each person)

 Other items:
- paper plates (50 plates; $3.50)
- paper cups (100 cups; $2.75)
- napkins (200 napkins; $3.00)
- fancy balloons ($2.00 each)
- streamers (100 feet long; $1.75 each)

Starting a Business

Understanding the Student Perspective

Children see businesses all around them: stores, restaurants, doctors' offices, newspapers, plumbers, farms, architects, car washes, hotels, laundromats, sports teams, and factories. They may think of the business as the building that it's in rather than the people who work inside it, providing services or making goods. Online businesses may be even harder to conceive of. But anyone with a skill or a good idea can make money with it, even a child. When a child starts his or her own business, the benefits go well beyond any money he or she earns. Starting a business helps promote creativity, goal setting, a responsible work ethic, and an appreciation of money and its value. It also builds people skills and problem-solving skills.

This unit helps students understand the process of starting a business. The math skills used in this unit include addition, subtraction, multiplication, and using currency.

Pacing/Lesson Plan

1. Distribute a copy of A Cool Product on pages 92 and 93 to each student. Decide if you will have students read it in small groups or as a whole class. Note that the bold words in the story are defined on page 94.

2. Use the Discussion Questions on page 91 to lead a discussion with the class after reading A Cool Product.

3. Distribute a copy of Business Vocabulary on page 94 to each student. Introduce the vocabulary words, rephrasing or explaining as needed. Then have students complete the activity.

4. Distribute a copy of My Big Idea on page 95 to each student. Provide support as needed as students complete the activity.

5. Distribute a copy of What Could They Do? on page 96 to each student. Provide support as needed as students complete the activity.

6. Distribute a copy of Name That Business on page 97 to each student. Provide support as needed as students complete the activity.

7. Distribute a copy of Small Business, Big Dream on page 98 to each student. Make play money or counters available for students. Provide support as needed as students complete the activity.

8. Distribute a copy of Profit or No Profit? on page 99 to each student. Make play money or counters available for students. Provide support as needed as students complete the activity.

9. Have students do the Let's Start a Business activity on page 100. To prepare, make copies of Our Business Plan on page 101 for each group. Gather the other needed materials. After groups have created their signs, display them in the classroom. Allow groups offering similar products or services to compare their prices and think about how they could compete for consumers' business.

Discussion Questions

Use these questions to lead a discussion with the class after reading the story. Feel free to rephrase these or add your own questions.

- What does Sanjay want to do to make money? *[make and sell birdhouses]*

- What type of business do Sanjay's grandparents own? *[a shoe shop]*

- Have you ever taken a risk? What kind? What happened?

- Do you know anyone who runs a business? Tell about it.

- Do you have any ideas for your own business?

 Materials

For word problems on pages 98 and 99:
- play money (see page 10)
- counters (optional)

For Let's Start a Business on pages 100 and 101—each group of 3 students needs:
- Our Business Plan, page 101
- Internet access
- a sheet of paper or poster board
- a pencil
- colored pencils, crayons, or markers

 Vocabulary Words

consumer	employee	entrepreneur	expense
product	profit	risk	

A Cool Product

Sanjay climbed onto the school bus and sat next to his friend Isabella. "I have a great idea! You know those two birdhouses we made with my dad? Let's make more and sell them!"

Isabella said, "I love that idea! But first, we need to make a good business plan."

Sanjay pretended to look confused for a second. Then he responded, "Here's a good plan. We have a cool **product**. Let's just make a whole bunch and sell them."

Isabella knew she should have explained first. "The plan isn't to decide *what* we want to do but *how.*" Now Sanjay looked confused for real. Isabella continued, "We should figure out what **expenses** we'll have, how much they'll cost, and how much we want to charge for each birdhouse. That's the kind of planning an **entrepreneur** needs to do to run a business."

"Well, let's charge $100 each!" Sanjay stated. "We'll be rich!"

Isabella laughed. "**Consumers** might not want to pay that much. Would you?" Sanjay had to admit that he probably wouldn't. That's a lot of money!

"Let's think about what we need to buy to build a birdhouse—wood, nails, and glue," Isabella said. "What did your dad spend to make each birdhouse?"

Sanjay thought back to his trip to the hardware store with his father. He thought Dad paid about $30 there. "I think he spent $15 for each," Sanjay said.

Isabella was calculating. "So, if we sell our birdhouses for a reasonable price, maybe $40, the **profit** will be $25 on each one."

Sanjay was thinking about how long it took to make one. Was all that time worth $25? It took a long time to rub the cut edges with sandpaper to make them smooth, even though it was easy to do. Then he had another great idea. "Oh! Let's hire my little brother to help with sanding. That will make it go faster."

Name _____

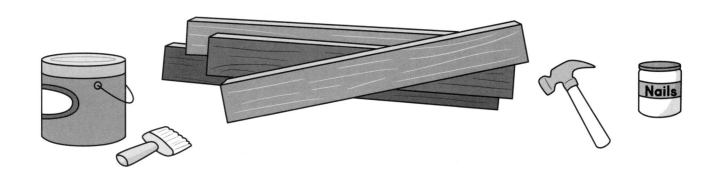

Isabella agreed that the work would go faster, but then they'd have an **employee**. They would need to pay him. Then they'd earn even less than $25 for each birdhouse.

Sanjay said, "Hmmm. Let's start with just the two of us. We can buy supplies this Saturday. Let's make 10 birdhouses to start."

Isabella said, "That's a lot of birdhouses! What if nobody buys one?"

Sanjay shrugged his shoulders as they pulled into the school parking lot. "You take a **risk** when you start a business. But if things go well, it'll be worth it."

Isabella said, "Supplies for 10 birdhouses will cost $150. That's a lot of money. Do you have that much to spend?"

Sanjay said he'd have to check. "I suppose we might need another plan to get that much."

Isabella said, "Yes, we would. That plan might be getting a loan. Do you think you could borrow the money from your dad?"

"Maybe," Sanjay said, "and if he won't help us, I can ask my grandparents for a loan. They own a shoe shop in their city. I think they'd like to help their grandson get started in business."

"That's a great idea!" said Isabella. "They can look at our plans and tell us what they think! Maybe they'll have some good ideas."

Sanjay laughed. "Talking to my grandparents might just be the best plan of all!"

Name _____

Business Vocabulary

1. Read the word. Read the definition.
2. Find the word in A Cool Product and read the sentence.
3. Then write your own sentence below using the word.

consumer   a person who buys goods and services

_____

employee   someone who is paid to do a job

_____

entrepreneur   a person who starts his or her own business

_____

expense   something you pay for

_____

product   something that is made and then sold

_____

profit   the amount of money left over after buying supplies
and paying workers

_____

risk   the possibility of losing something or being harmed

_____

Financial Literacy Lessons and Activities • EMC 3124 • © Evan-Moor Corporation

My Big Idea

Read the journal entry. Write the vocabulary word from the word box to complete each sentence. Then read the entry again.

Word Box

consumers   employee   entrepreneur   expenses   product   profit   risk

---

September 20, 2823

My new home, Zax, is on an interesting planet. It has even more water than

Earth. All this water gave me an idea for a new business. So I decided to become

an _____. My new _____ is called Zip Boat.

Of course, there are already a lot of boats on Zax. But my boat is smaller and

faster than all the others. I think _____ will buy it. I found a

company that makes boat parts with natural materials. I plan to buy all my

supplies from them. I even hired an _____ to help me. I'm a little

worried about the _____ that comes with starting a business like

this. But I have a good business plan. I'll have to spend quite a bit of money on

_____ at first. But if everything goes well, I'll start earning a great

_____ after one year. Who knows? Maybe someday, Zip Boat

will be the most popular boat on the planet!

Name _____

What Could They Do?

Many entrepreneurs take something they love to do and turn it into a business. Read about the skills and interests of the people below. Then write one or more ways they could use their talents to make money. There are no right or wrong answers.

1. Petros likes to cook. He also likes to eat. He takes photos and likes to be in front of a video camera as often as possible.

   How could Petros turn these skills and interests into a business?

   _____

   _____

   _____

2. Rachel loves to build things with wood. She carves wood, too. She likes to draw and use tools. She knows about many different kinds of trees. She is very creative.

   How could Rachel turn these skills and interests into a business?

   _____

   _____

   _____

3. Neeti plays guitar and piano. She enjoys working with kids. She loves to perform. She knows a lot of other musicians, too.

   How could Neeti turn these skills and interests into a business?

   _____

   _____

Name _____

Name That Business

When you start your own business, you need to give it a catchy name. It should get people's attention. It should also give people an idea of what it does.

Read each business idea. Write a catchy name for the business. There are no right or wrong answers.

1. Trey is opening a pizza restaurant in New York City. Each pizza features flavors and ingredients from different countries. There are pizzas from India, Mexico, Ethiopia, and many other places. If a customer ate all the pizzas on the menu, it would be like traveling around the world!

_____

2. Berta carves bird shapes out of wood. She also makes bird jewelry, bird cellphone stands, and even eyeglass holders that are shaped like birds. She plans to start selling them. Berta first fell in love with birds when she was six years old and her grandfather took her bird-watching.

_____

3. Juan is going to start an after-school soccer program for kids. He used to play soccer professionally. Now he wants to share his passion for the sport with others. He especially enjoys how players work together as a team. He believes that everyone who works hard will be successful.

_____

Name _____

Small Business, Big Dream

Layla loves animals. She wants to be a veterinarian someday. To learn more about animals and make some money, she starts a pet-care business. Read each word problem. Write your answers.

1. Layla gives baths to dogs and cats. She charges $8.25 for each bath. For each bath, she uses 75¢ worth of shampoo. What is Layla's profit for each bath?

   $ _____

2. Layla walks dogs as part of her business. She charges $5.00 an hour for each dog. She spent $13.50 on dog treats. How many hours does she need to work to start earning a profit walking dogs?

   _____

3. Layla has an idea for a new cat toy. To make the toy, she needs the following supplies:

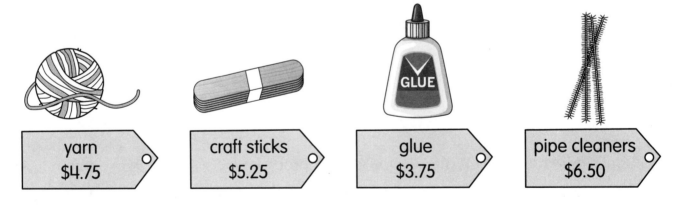

| yarn | craft sticks | glue | pipe cleaners |
| $4.75 | $5.25 | $3.75 | $6.50 |

   How much money does Layla need to start making cat toys?

   $ _____

4. Layla does pet sitting in her home for $12.00 a day. This summer, she has 36 days of pet sitting appointments on her calendar. How much money will Layla earn?

   $ _____

Name _____

Profit or No Profit?

To earn money, a business must pay for supplies and pay its employees. A business makes a profit only when it makes more money than it spends.

Terry and Chris started a business making fliers and greeting cards. For each job they took, they wrote down how much they earned and how much they spent. Use the table to compare what they earned and spent for each job and the total. Write **yes** or **no** to show if they made a profit.

Job	Earned	Spent		Profit?
		Supplies	**Employees**	
1	$30.50	$18.75	$0	
2	$48.75	$19.25	$30.50	
3	$100.00	$86.50	$10.25	
4	$53.75	$24.75	$22.25	
5	$78.25	$39.25	$39.50	
6	$35.00	$17.00	$16.75	
7	$65.00	$0	$72.50	
Total	$411.25	$205.50	$191.75	

Let's Start a Business

You will work in a small group to gather cost information for a business idea.

WHAT YOU NEED

- Our Business Plan, page 101
- Internet access
- colored pencils, crayons, or markers
- a sheet of paper or poster board
- a pencil

WHAT YOU DO

1. Get into groups of 3 students.

2. Make a list of skills that each person in your group has. Write them on Our Business Plan.

3. Think about how the skills could be used to make a product or provide a service. Circle the things that people might need or want. Choose one for your business. Think of a business name. Describe what your business will sell or do.

4. Think about the most important supplies or tools you would need for your business and list them. Then use the Internet to find a cost for anything you would need to buy. For supplies, which will be used up, write the quantity with the cost (for example, $2.00 for 90 nails).

5. Look at the costs. Think about how many of each thing you'll need to make your product or do your service. Also think about how long it will take you to make the product or do the service. Decide on a price to charge for your product or service.

6. Create a sign for your product or service. Share it with your class. If any other groups chose the same product or service as your group, compare those prices with yours. Think about how your business could compete with any other groups offering the same thing.

Our Business Plan

Skills in our group:

[ ]

Our business name: _____

What we sell or do: _____

_____

Costs of Supplies or Tools:

_____ $_____

_____ $_____

_____ $_____

_____ $_____

Selling Prices of Goods or Services:

_____ $_____

_____ $_____

_____ $_____

Paying Bills

 Understanding the Student Perspective

For children, spending money usually involves fun things or items they want. They rarely have any financial responsibilities and may not realize how much all the modern conveniences we enjoy cost or how often they must be paid. These include housing, electricity, water, and heat. People often have other bills, too, such as cable or Internet, garbage collection, gym memberships, subscriptions, and various types of home maintenance, such as lawn care or housecleaning.

This unit makes students aware of how we pay for "home infrastructure": the home and all the services in it. The math skills used in this unit include addition, subtraction, multiplication, division, and using currency.

 Pacing/Lesson Plan

1. Distribute a copy of Another Streaming Service on pages 104 and 105 to each student. Decide if you will have students read it in small groups or as a whole class. Note that the bold words in the story are defined on page 106.

2. Use the Discussion Questions on page 103 to lead a discussion with the class after reading Another Streaming Service.

3. Distribute a copy of Paying Bills Vocabulary on page 106 to each student. Introduce the vocabulary words, rephrasing or explaining as needed. Then have students complete the activity.

4. Distribute a copy of Paying Bills Crossword Puzzle on page 107 to each student. Provide support as needed as students complete the activity.

5. Distribute a copy of Sadiq's Services on page 108 to each student. Provide support as needed as students complete the activity.

6. Distribute a copy of Fast, Easy, or Cheap? on page 109 to each student. Provide support as needed as students complete the activity.

7. Distribute a copy of Carolina's Bills on page 110 to each student. Make play money or counters available for students. Provide support as needed as students complete the activity.

8. Distribute a copy of Ty Pays for Power on page 111 to each student. Make play money or counters available for students. Provide support as needed as students complete the activity.

9. Have students play The Paying Path on page 112. To prepare, make copies of the Game Board on page 113 for each group. Gather the other needed materials.

Discussion Questions

Use these questions to lead a discussion with the class after reading the story. Feel free to rephrase these or add your own questions.

- How many streaming services did Aixa and her dad subscribe to? Why did Aixa want to subscribe to another one? *[three; she wanted to watch a show on another one.]*

- What are some examples of utilities? Why do we need them? *[electricity, heat, water, phone, TV, trash pickup, Internet; they make our lives easier]*

- Other than utilities and rent or mortgage, what bills do you think your parents pay each month? Do you have any of your own bills?

- What bills do you think you'll pay when you have your own house or apartment? How do you think you will feel spending your money on things like electricity or heat?

 Materials

For word problems on pages 110 and 111:
- play money (see page 10)
- counters (optional)

For The Paying Path on pages 112 and 113—each group of 4 students needs:
- Game Board, page 113
- play money (see page 10)
- a die
- distinct game pieces (beads, coins, buttons, or other small objects)

 Vocabulary Words

autopay	bill	monthly	mortgage
rent	subscribe	utility	waste management

Another Streaming Service

"Dad!" Aixa said. "We need to **subscribe** to TV Plus! It has a new show called *Nitro Runner*!"

"We already subscribe to three," Dad responded. "We don't need another streaming service."

"But they don't have *Nitro Runner,*" Aixa said.

"Sorry," Dad said, shaking his head, "but I don't need another **bill** to pay each month."

Aixa scratched her head. "What other bills do we have?"

Dad chuckled as he clicked off the TV and then picked up his phone and read a text message. "Every part of this house that does something—it all costs money."

"What do you mean?" Aixa asked. "I thought you bought this house so you wouldn't have to pay **rent** every month."

"Houses cost a lot! Most people need a special loan, called a **mortgage**, to help pay for it," Dad explained. "A bank paid for the house. We are paying back to the bank part of what we owe every month. We also pay a **monthly** bill for each **utility**, such as electric, heat, water, and **waste management**."

"Those things aren't even fun, especially garbage pickup," Aixa said, wrinkling her nose. "It's too bad we have to pay for all that."

Dad laughed. "That stuff isn't fun. But it makes our life much easier. Remember when the power went out for a few hours last summer?"

"Oh, that was awful!" she recalled. "There was no air conditioning, and we couldn't even play video games."

"Right," Dad said, "and we didn't want to open the refrigerator door because we were afraid the food might spoil in the heat. And it's not just our home. Imagine not having a car."

Paying Bills

"We wouldn't be able to get to the store," Aixa said, "or to the gym or to my piano lessons."

"Well, we could buy bus passes," Dad said, "which would be another bill."

"It's a good thing we own a car then," Aixa said. "I guess the gym membership and my piano lessons are other bills you pay for, right?"

"Yes," Dad said.

"Wow, Dad, you must spend a lot of time paying all those bills. When do you have time to work?" Aixa joked.

Dad laughed. "I have most of them on **autopay**. The money is sent from our bank account automatically to pay them."

"In that case, do you want to go jogging with me?" Aixa asked. "If I can't watch *Nitro Runner,* maybe I can become one!"

"Yes, I'd love to spend some time with my clever daughter!" Dad said as he sat down to put on his running shoes.

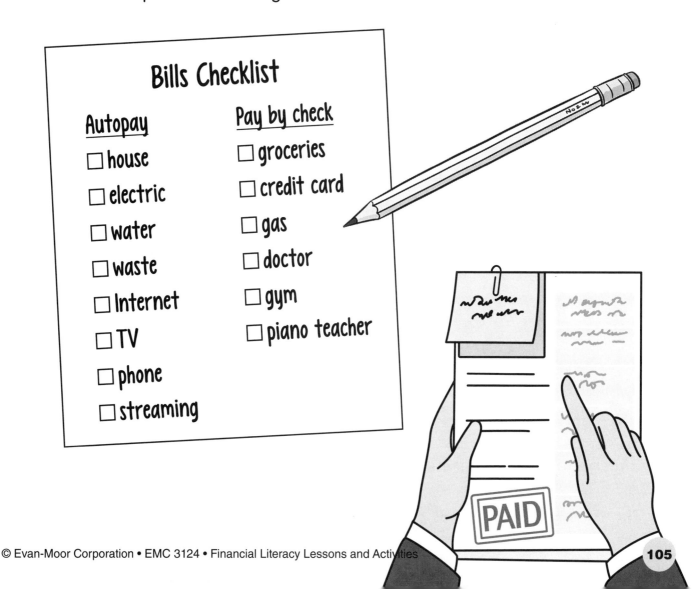

Bills Checklist

Autopay
- ☐ house
- ☐ electric
- ☐ water
- ☐ waste
- ☐ Internet
- ☐ TV
- ☐ phone
- ☐ streaming

Pay by check
- ☐ groceries
- ☐ credit card
- ☐ gas
- ☐ doctor
- ☐ gym
- ☐ piano teacher

PAID

Name _____

Paying Bills Vocabulary

1. Read the word or term. Read the definition.
2. Find the word in Another Streaming Service and read the sentence.
3. Then write your own sentence below using the word or term.

autopay   a service that takes money from an account to pay a bill

_____

bill   an amount of money that must be paid for a service

_____

monthly   happening once a month

_____

mortgage   a loan that someone gets to buy a house

_____

rent   money paid every month to use something owned by someone else

_____

subscribe   to sign up for and receive an information or entertainment service

_____

utility   a service, such as power or water, that a household needs

_____

waste management   a service that collects garbage and recycling

_____

Financial Literacy Lessons and Activities • EMC 3124 • © Evan-Moor Corporation

Name _____

Paying Bills Crossword Puzzle

Find the vocabulary word or term that completes the sentence. Then write it in the crossword.

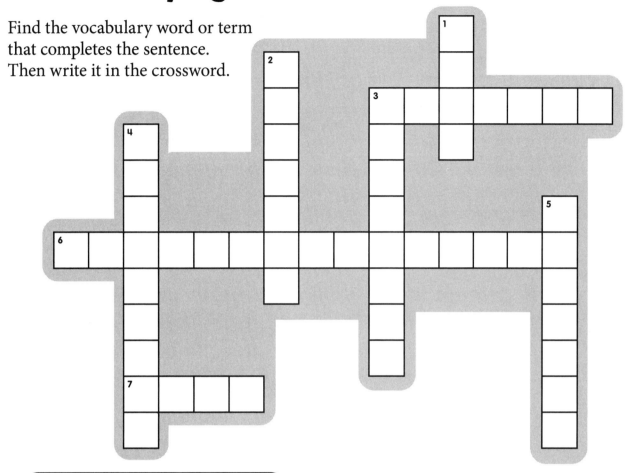

Word Box

autopay	bill	monthly
mortage	rent	subscribe
utility	waste management	

Across

3. Bills that are paid _____ are paid twelve times a year.

6. If it weren't for the _____ company, we'd be buried in trash!

7. If you don't pay the cable _____, you can't watch your favorite TV show.

Down

1. My parents _____ a car when we visit my cousins in Montana.

2. I set up my bills for _____ so I won't forget to pay them.

3. My grandparents just finished paying off the _____ on their house.

4. Which music-streaming service do you _____ to?

5. A water park isn't a _____, but the company that provides water to the park is.

Name _____

Sadiq's Services

Sadiq has a problem. He has too many bills! He wants to save some money.

Look at Sadiq's monthly bills below. Draw a line through the services that you think he could do without. Circle the services that he still needs. There are no right or wrong answers.

Fit Planet Gym membership	$45
True Savings Bank (mortgage)	$1,051
East City Water	$79
Green's Lawn-Mowing Service	$160
Mrs. Sparkle's Housecleaning Service	$200
East City Electric Company	$316
Internet	$86
TV Plus streaming service #1	$9
Top Movies streaming service #2	$7
Diego's Pest Control	$90
Cozy's Heating Oil (for heat)	$60
Gotta Watch streaming service #3	$8

   Financial Literacy Lessons and Activities • EMC 3124 • © Evan-Moor Corporation

Name _____

Fast, Easy, or Cheap?

There are different ways to get some tasks done. But sometimes people must make a choice: give up time, convenience, or money.

Read the options below. For each pair, imagine that you earn enough money to afford either option. Circle which option you would choose. Explain your answer. There are no right or wrong answers.

Option #1: pay $65 each month for a gym membership

Option #2: buy exercise equipment for $200 and work out at home

_____

_____

_____

Option #1: pay $150 each month for a housecleaning service

Option #2: clean your home yourself

_____

_____

_____

Option #1: pay $200 each month for a lawn-mowing service

Option #2: buy a lawn mower for $300 and mow your lawn yourself

_____

_____

_____

Name _____

Carolina's Bills

Read each word problem. Write your answers.

1. Carolina pays $8.75 each month for her favorite streaming service. How much does she pay each year?

   $ _____

2. Last month, Carolina's electric bill was $122.25. This month it was $163.50. How much more was Carolina's electric bill this month?

   $ _____

3. Carolina has three bills to pay today: a water bill for $47.75, a monthly gym membership for $29.50, and an Internet bill for $55.00. How much money will Carolina spend today to pay all three bills?

   $ _____

4. Carolina had to rent a car for 9 days while her car was being repaired. The car-rental company gave her a bill for $405.00. How much did the car cost each day?

   $ _____

  Financial Literacy Lessons and Activities • EMC 3124 • © Evan-Moor Corporation

Name _____

Ty Pays for Power

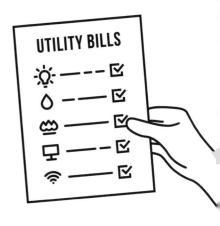

Read each word problem. Write your answers.

1. In January, Ty's heating bill was $92.50. His electric bill was $19.25 more than that. How much was his electric bill?

$_____

2. For February, Ty's heating bill was $78.00. For March, his heating bill was $83.10. For April, his heating bill was $68.60. How much did Ty spend on heating February through April?

$_____

3. Ty's electric bill in May was $132.10. In June, he started using the air conditioner. His bill for June was $181.75. How much more did it cost him to use his air conditioner?

$_____

4. Ty subscribes to three streaming services. TV Plus is $4.50 a month. Star Time is $8.25 a month. Hit Movies is $6.50 a month. Ty plans to spend more time outside now that the weather is warm. How much money will he save each month if he cancels all three subscriptions?

$_____

Name _____

The Paying Path

In this game, players try to be the first to pay all their monthly bills. Along the way, players can spend money on fun things. But beware: If you run out of money, you have to start over!

SETUP

- Get into groups of 4 players. Choose one player to be the banker.

- Gather materials: copies of the Game Board, page 113; dice; game pieces; play money (page 10)

- Each group gets a Game Board and a die.

- Each player gets a game piece and $120.

PLAY

The object of the game is to end up with enough money to pay all your bills.

Place the game pieces on the START space on the Game Board.

On each turn, a player rolls the die and moves his or her game piece the same number of spaces.

If the space that the player lands on **costs** money, the player has two choices:

- Spend the money.

- Don't spend the money and move backward. To find out how far back to go, roll the die. Go back that many spaces.

A player who lands on Pay Day! collects $25.

If a player runs out of money, he or she can return to START and collect $120.

The first player to reach the Monthly bills space at the end with enough money to pay all three bills wins. If the player reaches the space without enough money, he or she can return to START and collect $120.

Paying Bills

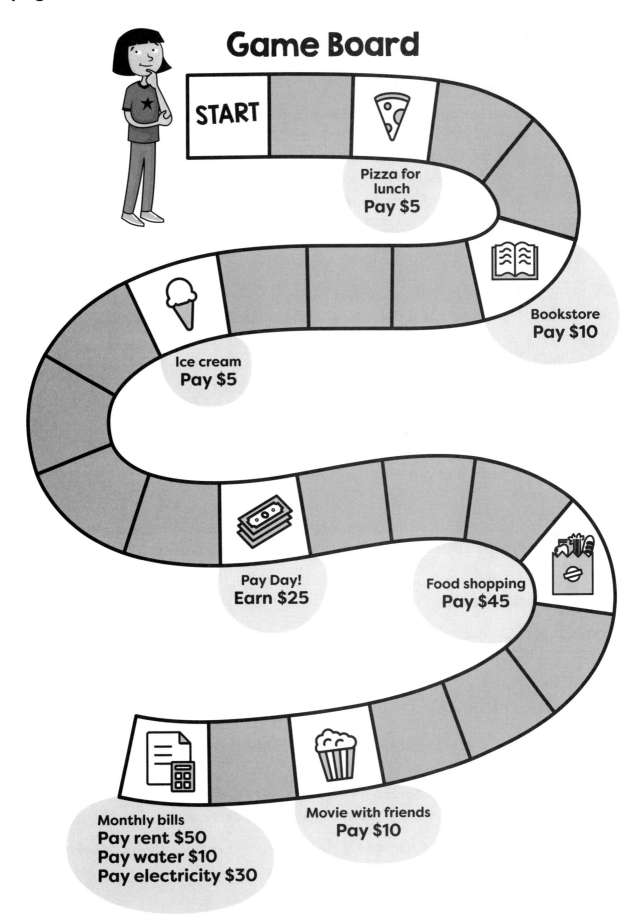

Game Board

START

Pizza for
lunch
Pay $5

Bookstore
Pay $10

Ice cream
Pay $5

Pay Day!
Earn $25

Food shopping
Pay $45

Monthly bills
Pay rent $50
Pay water $10
Pay electricity $30

Movie with friends
Pay $10

Using Credit Cards

Understanding the Student Perspective

A credit card may seem like free money to a child. Paying with cash is very concrete; you know how much you have, and after you pay for something, that money is gone. Using a credit card is more abstract; after you pay, you still have the credit card. From a child's point of view, it may seem unlimited. Paying with a credit card is like receiving a small loan that must be paid back. To use one responsibly, a person should know how much money he or she has in the bank and how much money to expect in the future. A person who is not careful with a credit card can wind up with more debt than he or she can ever pay off. Teaching children about credit can help ensure they avoid making such mistakes in the future.

This unit helps students understand how credit cards work and how to use them safely. The math skills used in this unit include addition, subtraction, multiplication, and using currency.

Pacing/Lesson Plan

1. Distribute a copy of A New Refrigerator on pages 116 and 117 to each student. Decide if you will have students read it in small groups or as a whole class. Note that the bold words in the story are defined on page 118.

2. Use the Discussion Questions on page 115 to lead a discussion with the class after reading A New Refrigerator.

3. Distribute a copy of Credit Card Vocabulary on page 118 to each student. Introduce the vocabulary words, rephrasing or explaining as needed. Then have students complete the activity.

4. Distribute a copy of Getting Outdoors on page 119 to each student. Provide support as needed as students complete the activity.

5. Distribute a copy of Cheaper or Faster? on page 120 to each student. Provide support as needed as students complete the activity.

6. Distribute a copy of Making a Statement on page 121 to each student. Provide support as needed as students complete the activity.

7. Distribute a copy of Zooey's Credit Card on page 122 to each student. Make play money or counters available for students. Provide support as needed as students complete the activity.

8. Distribute a copy of Credit Card Statements on page 123 to each student. Make play money or counters available for students. Provide support as needed as students complete the activity.

9. Have students play Get Out of Debt! on page 124. To prepare, make copies of the Game Board on page 125 for each group. Gather the other needed materials.

Discussion Questions

Use these questions to lead a discussion with the class after reading the story. Feel free to rephrase these or add your own questions.

- Why did Ryu's mom buy the new refrigerator using credit? *[She didn't have enough money saved up yet.]*

- Why do you think credit card companies charge interest?

- How do you think a credit card can be helpful?

- Do you think it is good that credit cards have a limit? Why?
  What might happen if they did **not** limit how much you spent?

 Materials

For word problems on pages 122 and 123:
- play money (see page 10)
- counters (optional)

For Get Out of Debt! on pages 124 and 125—each group of 3 or 4 students needs:
- Game Board, page 125
- play money (see page 10)
- a die
- distinct game pieces (beads, coins, buttons, or other small objects)

 Vocabulary Words

credit	debt	interest	limit
minimum	statement	transaction	

A New Refrigerator

On Saturday morning, Ryu opened the refrigerator. His eyes went wide. The air inside it was warm.

"Uh-oh," he said. He woke up his mom.

When Mom saw the refrigerator, she sighed. "That's the third time this month. It looks like it's time to replace it," she said. "That won't be cheap."

Ryu bit his lip. They were supposed to get him some new soccer cleats. "How will we buy my new cleats and a new refrigerator?" he asked. "That'll be a lot of money."

"Don't worry," Mom said. "We can pay for both with **credit**."

Later that morning, they went to the shopping center. At the home-improvement store, Mom picked out a refrigerator with some new features that their old one didn't have.

"We can deliver it later this afternoon," a salesperson said.

"I'm glad to hear that!" Mom said.

"Would you like to pay with cash or credit?" the salesperson asked.

Mom took out her credit card. "Credit, please." Then she put her credit card in the reader and signed her name on the screen to finish the **transaction**.

Next, they went to the sporting goods store. Ryu found a pair of soccer cleats. Mom tried on a running jacket and decided to buy it.

Ryu watched his mom use her credit card.

"It's like free money," Ryu said. "We could buy everything in the store!"

"Very funny," Mom said. "There's a **limit** on this credit card. We can't buy everything. Plus, it's not free money. Credit is like a loan. You can buy things with it, but you must pay back the money."

"I know," Ryu said. "You get that credit card **statement** in the mail each month. Plus, we get all that junk mail about credit cards and **interest** rates. What is interest anyway?"

"Interest is one of the ways credit card companies make money," Mom said. "The credit card company is helping us out by paying for our items so we can have them now. Interest is what we pay for that help."

Ryu was starting to understand. "Is it like when you pay Mr. Anaya to mow our lawn?" he asked. "You pay him so we can have a nice lawn sooner?"

Mom laughed. "I guess so! Lending money and mowing lawns are both services that we pay for. They make our lives a little easier. But there is a difference," she noted. "When we pay Mr. Anaya, we are done. When we use a credit card, we have **debt**, or money that we owe."

"How fast do we have to pay it back?" Ryu asked.

"That's up to us. We can pay it back quickly or slowly. We just have to make at least the **minimum** payment each month," Mom said. "However, the longer we take, the more interest we pay."

"Oh, I guess we don't want to take very long then," Ryu said. "How much is the interest?"

"It depends on the cost of what you buy and how long you take to pay it back," Mom replied.

Ryu thought about the refrigerator. It had cost almost $1,200. "We'll have to pay a lot of interest on the fridge, right?" he asked.

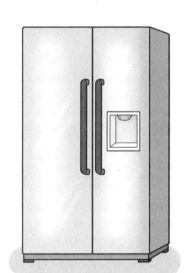

"I'll pay it back over the next 12 months," Mom answered. "The interest will be around $130. I know that's a lot. But the convenience of having a credit card makes it worth it. If I did not have a credit card, we wouldn't be able to replace our refrigerator until we had saved up enough money."

Ryu grinned. "We probably have enough money to stop for ice cream, right?"

Laughing, Mom shook her head. "Nice try, Ryu. Our new refrigerator will be delivered soon. Then we'll go shopping to put some fresh food inside it!"

Name _____

Credit Card Vocabulary

1. Read the word. Read the definition.
2. Find the word in A New Refrigerator and read the sentence.
3. Then write your own sentence below using the word.

credit   an amount of money that can be spent now and paid back later

_____

debt   money that someone owes

_____

interest   money made by lending money or paid to borrow money

_____

limit   the highest amount allowed

_____

minimum   the smallest amount

_____

statement   a report that tells how much money has been used

_____

transaction   a trade of goods or services for money

_____

Getting Outdoors

Read the story. Edit it by replacing each bold phrase with the correct vocabulary word from the word box. Then read the story again.

Word Box

credit	debt	interest	limit
minimum	statement	transaction	

The other day, I went to the store to buy a mountain bike. This would have

been the biggest _____ that I had ever made.
trade of money for something

But the bike I wanted was over the _____ on
highest amount I could spend

my credit card. So instead, I bought a backpack for hiking. I still

paid with _____ . Of course, now
money that is available to spend

I have some _____ . When I get my
money that I owe

_____ , I'll decide how much I can pay back right
report showing how much I spent

away. Hopefully, I'll be able to pay it all back in a few months. If I make only the

_____ payment, the _____
smallest **money I owe for using credit**

will really add up!

Using Credit Cards

Name _____

Cheaper or Faster?

Credit cards are helpful if you need to buy something expensive but don't have enough money right now. Credit cards also make buying things easy since you don't need to carry a bunch of cash. You must pay back the money you charge to a credit card. If you don't pay the money back right away, you must also pay interest.

Using a credit card is a way to borrow money. The credit card company buys the item for you. Then you pay the credit card company back. You are responsible for the cost.

Read each story. Then decide if you would use a credit card or cash. Circle the one you choose and explain why you chose that way to pay. There are no right or wrong answers.

1. Jake's mom wants four new outfits with jewelry for her new job. Here are her choices:

Using a credit card	Saving up to buy with cash
cost: $1,166	**cost:** $968
when she can get it: now	**when she can get it:** in 4 months

Explain: _____

_____

_____

2. Heidi's dad's car broke down while he was driving to work. He has to rent a car while his own car is being repaired. Here are his choices to pay for the car repair:

Using a credit card	Saving up to buy with cash
cost: $2,721	**cost:** $2,259
when he can get it: now	**when he can get it:** in 6 months

Explain: _____

_____

_____

Name _____

Making a Statement

Erik used his credit card to buy several things this month. He has a receipt for each transaction. At the end of the month, the credit card company sent Erik a statement showing all the transactions, the current balance that he owes, and his minimum payment due.

Use Erik's receipts to complete the statement below. Then imagine that you are Erik. Write the amount that you think he should pay. You can choose to pay any amount as long as it isn't lower than the minimum payment due.

Connor's Clothing Looking cool in Connor's	
jacket	$38.49
pants	$42.99
Total:	**$81.48**
*******3456	
May 4, 2023	

	May 11, 2023
FuelFill Gas Station	
15 gal.	$5.29 a gal.
Total:	**$79.35**
credit card sale	
**********3456 approved	

Showtime Theater Snack Shop	
May 20, '23	7:32 p.m.
credit ***********3456	
1 lg popcorn	$9.99
2 med soda	$8.60
Total:	**$18.59**

Safe Savers Bank   **May 2023 Statement**

Account holder: Erik Evan   1234 5678 9012 3456

Activity

May 4	Connor's Clothing	$_____
May 11	_____	$79.35
_____	Showtime Theater	$18.59
	Total:	**$179.42**

Minimum payment due: $25.00

Amount paid: $_____

Explain why you chose that amount to pay.

_____

_____

Name _____

Zooey's Credit Card

Read each word problem. Write your answers.

1. Zooey has a credit card with a credit limit of $600.00. She uses the card to buy a pair of wireless earbuds for $124.50. How much credit does she have left on the card? $_____

2. Zooey buys 6 new strings for her guitar. They cost $5.50 each. How much does she spend on guitar strings? $_____

3. Zooey uses her credit card to buy a snack for $3.80, a book for $11.95, and gum for $2.40. With the earbuds and guitar strings, how much debt does she have now? $_____

4. The minimum payment due on Zooey's credit card statement is $17.60. She makes only the minimum payment. How much more money does she still owe? $_____

5. The following month, Zooey's credit card company adds an interest fee of $28.45 to the amount she owes. How much will Zooey owe that month if she does not use her credit card to buy anything else? $_____

Name _____

Credit Card Statements

Credit card companies send a statement to each account holder each month. Look at the sample statement and what each part means.

Previous Balance	$100.00	Debt from last month
Payment	–$10.00	Amount paid last month
Interest Charged	+$9.00	Fee for unpaid previous balance
Purchases	+$20.00	Total spent this month
New Balance	$119.00	Debt for this month

For each statement, figure out the new balance.

1.

Previous Balance	$50.00
Payments	–$20.00
Interest Charged	+$3.00
Purchases	+$0.00
New Balance	$_____

2.

Previous Balance	$79.00
Payments	–$39.00
Interest Charged	+$6.00
Purchases	+$20.00
New Balance	$_____

3.

Previous Balance	$65.00
Payments	–$25.00
Interest Charged	+$5.00
Purchases	+$10.00
New Balance	$_____

4.

Previous Balance	$82.00
Payments	–$82.00
Interest Charged	+$0.00
Purchases	+$34.00
New Balance	$_____

Name _____

Get Out of Debt!

In this game, players try to pay off their credit card bill. But a roll of the die decides what they buy with their credit card!

> ## SETUP
>
> - Get into a group of 3 or 4. Choose one player to be the banker.
> - Gather materials: Game Board (page 125), play money, game pieces, 1 die
> - Players get $350 each. This is the debt that they must pay back to the bank.

PLAY

The object of the game is to become debt-free first.

Put the game pieces on Month 1 of the Game Board.

The first player rolls the die.

- Find the number that was rolled in the "What Happened?" part of the board.
- Read the words next to the number you rolled.

- If you use your credit card, the banker gives you the amount you need.
- If you can pay back some money, give it to the banker.
- Move your game piece to the next month.

Repeat for each player.

When all players have moved to the next month, everyone pays $60 of their debt to the banker.

Continue for all 8 months or until a player is debt-free (all money has been paid back to the bank).

If more than one person becomes debt-free in the same month, they both win.

If players reach the end of the board and nobody is debt-free, return all pieces to Month 1 and continue playing.

Game Board

Month 1	
Month 2	
Month 3	
Month 4	
Month 5	
Month 6	
Month 7	
Month 8	

What Happened?

⚀ You need to buy groceries. Charge $35 to your credit card.

⚁ Your dog needs to go to the vet. Charge $50 to your credit card.

⚂ You won $40! Use it to pay back your credit card debt.

⚃ You need new shoes. Charge $70 to your credit card.

⚄ You went to lunch with a friend. Charge $20 to your credit card.

⚅ You don't have any bills. Yay!

Pay the bank at the end of each month: $60

Paying for Health Services

Understanding the Student Perspective

Children will probably be familiar with going to the doctor, the dentist, and perhaps an eye doctor or other specialist, and they may have gone with a parent to the pharmacy to pick up a prescription. They may not be aware of the "behind-the-scenes" medical work, such as lab tests, taking and reading x-rays, and the development of medicines and medical devices, let alone the work of various kinds of therapists and mental health professionals. Even if children have seen parents paying something at the time of the visit, some of them might not be aware that additional costs may be billed later and that insurance may cover part of the cost.

This unit gives students a glimpse of the healthcare industry and the costs involved in staying healthy. The math skills used in this unit include addition, subtraction, multiplication, division, and using currency.

Pacing/Lesson Plan

1. Distribute a copy of Flying Through the Air on pages 128 and 129 to each student. Decide if you will have students read it in small groups or as a whole class. Note that the bold words in the story are defined on page 130.

2. Use the Discussion Questions on page 127 to lead a discussion with the class after reading Flying Through the Air.

3. Distribute a copy of Health Services Vocabulary on page 130 to each student. Introduce the vocabulary words, rephrasing or explaining as needed. Then have students complete the activity.

4. Distribute a copy of Health Services Riddles on page 131 to each student. Provide support as needed as students complete the activity.

5. Distribute a copy of Keeping Myself Healthy on page 132 to each student. Provide support as needed as students complete the activity.

6. Distribute a copy of Choosing Health Products on page 133 to each student. Provide support as needed as students complete the activity.

7. Distribute a copy of Mr. Wong's Medical Bills on page 134 to each student. Make play money or counters available for students. Provide support as needed as students complete the activity.

8. Distribute a copy of Ainsley Goes to the Drugstore on page 135 to each student. Make play money or counters available for students. Provide support as needed as students complete the activity.

9. Have students play A Path to Good Health on page 136. To prepare, make copies of the Game Board on page 137 for each group. Gather the other needed materials. After the students play, lead a class discussion on how the game reflects real life. [People might not have enough money for every treatment and may need to save for those that are more important.]

Discussion Questions

Use these questions to lead a discussion with the class after reading the story. Feel free to rephrase these or add your own questions.

- What injury did Ethan have? *[broken arm]*
  What procedure did he need? *[a cast put on]*

- Have you ever had a broken bone or been to an emergency room? Tell what happened.

- What do you think it would be like to be a doctor?

- Ethan's parents said that doctors and nurses are paid well. If a doctor or nurse were helping you, would you want him or her to be paid well? Why or why not?

 Materials

For word problems on pages 134 and 135:
- play money (see page 10)
- counters (optional)

For A Path to Good Health on pages 136 and 137—each group of 3 or 4 students needs:
- Game Board, page 137
- play money (see page 10)
- a die
- distinct game pieces (beads, coins, buttons, or other small objects)

 Vocabulary Words

appointment	copay	emergency room	insurance
prescription	procedure	surgery	therapy

Name _____

Flying Through the Air

I love mountain biking. But unfortunately, I won't be able to do it for a while. You see, there was this big rock, and I didn't see it. I went over my handlebars and . . . . You can guess the rest. Trust me—it was not fun!

I thought Mom would take me to my regular doctor. But no! She drove me to the **emergency room** instead. A doctor there took x-rays.

"Ethan," she said, "you have a broken arm."

I was shocked, but she said, "Don't worry—it's a small break, nothing serious." It was pretty sore. The doctor said that she would give me a **prescription** for pain medicine.

She put my arm in a brace. Then she gave my mom the name of a doctor who fixes bones. "Make an **appointment** with him tomorrow," she said.

We went to that doctor on Monday. Mom filled out lots of paperwork. She handed a card to the woman at the front desk.

"Your **insurance** pays for only part of this visit," the woman said. "You have a **copay** of $35."

Mom paid, and then we waited in the waiting room. Finally, I saw the doctor. "Good news!" he began. "I've looked at your x-rays, and you don't need **surgery**."

Paying for Health Services

That made me feel much better! Then he continued, "But I do want to do another **procedure**: I want to put a cast on your arm."

"Will that hurt?" I asked. "Will you have to dip me in cement?"

He laughed. "No! First, we'll wrap your arm in a cloth and some padding," he explained. "Then we'll apply plaster on cloth strips all around your arm very gently so we don't hurt your arm. After it starts to dry, you can go home."

That didn't sound too bad. I had signed my cousin's cast when she broke her leg skiing. She had to walk with crutches for a little while. "How soon can my friends sign my cast?" I asked.

"Wait two days until it is completely dried, and take it easy," the doctor warned. "No riding your bike, no sports, nothing active—keep your arm as still as you can."

That was a month ago. My cast came off today. I get to keep it, but guess what? I can't even pick it up with my healed arm. I can barely even move my arm! Now I have to get physical **therapy** to teach me exercises that will make it strong again.

I was shocked when I found out that my bike crash cost thousands of dollars. Mom and Dad told me that medical procedures cost a lot of money. Plus, doctors and nurses must go to school for a long time. They deserve to be paid well. Still, I felt bad that my accident cost so much.

"Don't be silly," they said. "Accidents happen. And besides, the insurance company paid for most of it. Now go enjoy yourself—safely!"

That made me feel better. But now I'll pay better attention to big rocks when I ride!

Name_____

Health Services Vocabulary

1. Read the word or term. Read the definition.
2. Find the word or term in Flying Through the Air and read the sentence.
3. Then write your own sentence below using the word or term.

appointment   a meeting that is set up ahead of time

_____

copay   a small charge for a doctor visit or medicine

_____

emergency room   the part of a hospital that provides medical care right away

_____

insurance   a service that helps pay expensive bills

_____

prescription   a note from a doctor for a specific medicine

_____

procedure   any treatment done to help fix an injury or illness

_____

surgery   fixing the body by cutting into it

_____

therapy   treatment to rebuild strength and ability

_____

Health Services Riddles

Read the riddle. Write the vocabulary word or term that completes the riddle.

> **Word Box**
>
> appointment   copay   emergency room   insurance
> prescription   procedure   surgery   therapy

1. During this _____, you'll be asleep. The doctor will work as you count sheep!

2. Good medical care can cost quite a lot. _____ will pay what you do not.

3. Did you fall down the stairs or slip in the snow? The _____ is the best place to go.

4. I'm glad there's no huge bill hanging over my head. I'm happy to pay my

   _____ instead.

5. My throat is sore. It hurts when I speak. I made an _____ with my doctor this week.

6. Your leg has been fixed; you're on the mend. Now you need _____ so your knee can bend.

7. I didn't want _____, but now that it's done, my insides feel great and are ready for fun.

8. I went to my doctor with a rash that made me scream.

   She wrote a _____ for a tube of cream.

Name _____

Keeping Myself Healthy

You need to go to a doctor for checkups and when you are sick or injured. If you take good care of yourself, you won't have to go as often. Think about ways to keep yourself healthy and safe. Write or draw at least 3 ways in each section below. There are no right or wrong answers.

FOOD I can eat…	**SAFETY** I can stay safe by…
EXERCISE I can stay active by…	**GERMS** I can avoid catching illnesses by…

Name _____

Choosing Health Products

When you are buying products, you usually have several options to choose from. There are many features to think about. Here are a few of them:

- Which one will work best?
- Which size is better?
- Which one will last longer?

- Which is the easiest to use?
- Which has the best price?
- Which is the newest product?

Read about some products and answer the items. There are no right or wrong answers.

1. Imagine that you are buying toothpaste. Read the information about each kind. Then circle your choice and explain why you chose it.

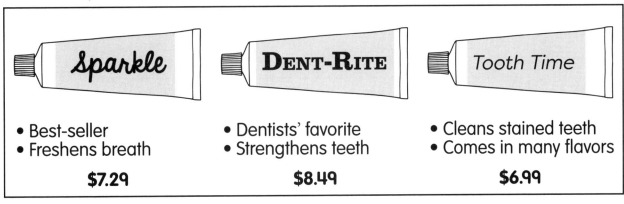

Sparkle
- Best-seller
- Freshens breath

$7.29

DENT-RITE
- Dentists' favorite
- Strengthens teeth

$8.49

Tooth Time
- Cleans stained teeth
- Comes in many flavors

$6.99

Explain: _____

_____

2. Imagine that you are buying vitamins. Read the information about each kind. Then circle your choice and explain why you chose it.

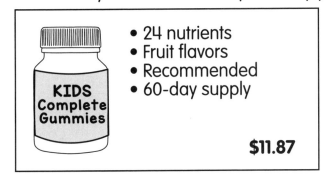

KIDS Complete Gummies
- 24 nutrients
- Fruit flavors
- Recommended
- 60-day supply

$11.87

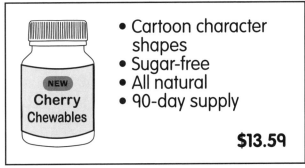

NEW Cherry Chewables
- Cartoon character shapes
- Sugar-free
- All natural
- 90-day supply

$13.59

Explain: _____

_____

Name _____

Mr. Wong's Medical Bills

Read about Mr. Wong's family's health insurance. Use it to answer each word problem. Write the answers in the table.

Silver Healthcare Plan

What Mr. Wong pays: $700 each month plus the part that insurance doesn't pay

What insurance pays:
- Emergency room: whole cost except for $125
- Surgery: whole cost except for $800
- Lab tests: half the cost

---

1. In April, Mrs. Wong went to the emergency room. It cost $8,942. How much did Mr. Wong and the insurance company spend in April?

2. In May, Mr. Wong's son had a medical test. It cost $850.00. How much did Mr. Wong and the insurance company spend in May?

3. In June, Mr. Wong needed surgery. It cost $1,375.00. How much did Mr. Wong and the insurance company spend in June?

4. How much did Mr. Wong and his insurance company pay in all from April through June?

	Mr. Wong	Insurance
April		
May		
June		
Total		

Name _____

Ainsley Goes to the Drugstore

Drugstores sell many things. You can buy prescription medicines that your doctor has ordered. You can also buy other products to help keep you healthy and make you feel better. Read and answer the questions about Ainsley's visit to the drugstore.

1. Ainsley wears sunscreen when she plays outside. Sunscreen helps prevent skin from getting sunburned.

Here are two choices: One tube has 6 ounces. The other has 3 ounces. Ainsley wants to buy 12 ounces of sunscreen for the whole summer. How much does 12 ounces of each cost?

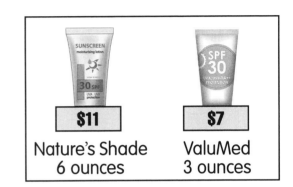

Nature's Shade $_____   ValuMed $_____

2. Ainsley has a cold. She buys these three products to make herself feel better.

How much does she spend for these cold products?

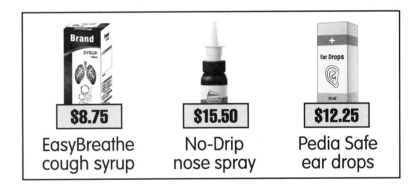

$_____

3. Ainsley injured her knee playing hockey. After three months of physical therapy, she was told to wear a knee brace when she played. She tried the Snug Support brace, but it didn't help much. The drugstore said that if she paid the difference in cost, she could trade it for the EnergX brace.

What was the difference in cost between the two knee braces?

$_____

A Path to Good Health

In this game, everyone who finishes with money left wins!

SETUP

- Get into groups of 3 or 4 players. Choose one player in each group to be the banker.

- Gather materials: copies of the Game Board (page 137), 1 die for each group, 1 game piece for each player, $100 in play money (page 10) for each player

---

PLAY

The object of the game is to reach the END space with money left.

All players place their game piece on the START space.

On each turn, a player rolls the die and moves his or her game piece the same number of spaces.

- Read the words in the space that the player lands on. Pay or get money as the space says.

- If a player doesn't have much money left, the player can choose to not pay and skip his or her next turn.

The game continues until each player runs out of money or reaches the END space.

A player does not have to roll the exact number to reach the end. For example, if a player is 3 spaces from the end and rolls a **4**, **5**, or **6**, that player moves to the END space.

All players who reach the END space with money left win.

Paying for Health Services

Game Board

You fell off your bike and need stitches.

Pay $40

Your feet itch. Buy foot spray.

Pay $13

Your stomach hurts. Doctor says to stay in bed.

No charge!

You've had a sore throat for three days. See the doctor.

Pay $50

The dentist says you need some fillings.

Pay $80

You hurt your wrist. Buy a wrist brace.

Pay $16

You have an ear infection. Buy a prescription medicine.

Pay $10

You had a good doctor checkup!

Pay $35 and move ahead 3 spaces!

You have a poison oak rash on your legs. Buy skin cream.

Pay $28

You were bit by a stray dog. Get a shot.

Pay $33

You may have a fever. Buy a thermometer.

Pay $12

You scraped your knee. Buy a box of bandages.

Pay $9

You stayed up too late and are tired. Take a nap.

No charge!

You lost your glasses. Buy another pair.

Pay $64

END

Answer Key

Buying at the Store

Page 23

1. discount
2. purchase
3. products
4. consumer
5. receipt
6. compare
7. debit card

Page 26

1.–3.

What was bought or sold in a month	How many	Cost for one	Cost for a month
50-pound bags of scratch	3	$18	$54
25-pound bags of scratch	6	$11	$66
cartons of eggs sold	15	$4	$60

4. no
5. yes

Page 27

1. $13.84; $1.16
2. $88.29; $90.00
3. $23.22; $6.90
4. $32.14; 60.04

Earning Money at a Job

Page 35

entrepreneur, business, responsibility, salary, raise, benefit

Page 38

1. $63.00
2. $4.50
3. 3 hours; $41.00
4. $10.50

Page 39

1.

	Hours a week	Hourly salary	Weekly salary
Art Studio Assistant	8	$8.00	$64.00
Gardener	4	$9.00	$36.00
Animal Rescue Helper	12	$7.00	$84.00

2.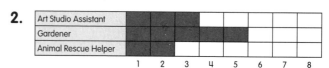

3. Answers will vary.

Making and Following a Budget

Using Banks

Page 47

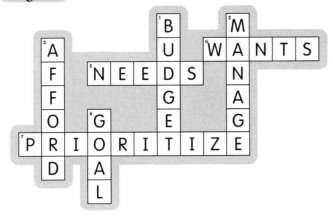

Page 59

Where no answer is shown, answers will vary.

It was a busy day at the bank today. A customer wanted to borrow money to

open a _____ store. He has had an ___account___ with the
adjective   vocabulary word

bank for _____ years, so we were happy to lend him the money.
number

Then a new customer asked a ___teller___ for help. She had just
vocabulary word

received her statement that showed every time she ___deposited___ money.
vocabulary word

She thought that the ___balance___ was too high. I told her that her money
vocabulary word

had earned some ___interest___. She was really _____ when
vocabulary word   emotion

she heard that!

The last customer of the day has a new job as a _____. He
job

held up his first paycheck and asked if it was more than the ___minimum___
vocabulary word

amount of money to open an account. It was! He was able to go to the

___ATM___ and ___withdraw___ $_____ from his
vocabulary word   vocabulary word   number

new bank account!

Page 50

Minh's Weekly Budget			
Earnings:	$ 45	Guitar lesson:	$ 10
Bank:	$ 15	Left over:	$ 14
Art class:	$ 6		

1. $15; $30
2. $14
3. 2 weeks

Page 62

1. $55.60
2. $60.75
3. $160.15
4. $1.90 OR 190¢; $191.90

Page 51

1.

Week	Earned	Spent	Saved
Week 1	$65	$25	$40
Week 2	$43	$25	$18
Week 3	$72	$25	$47
Week 4	$54	$25	$29
Week 5	$67	$25	$42
Week 6	$56	$25	$31

2. $357
3. $150
4. $207
5. $16.75
6. $8.25

Page 63

Action	Deposit	Withdraw	Balance
Starting balance			$65.00
Put in $2.00	+ $2.00		$67.00
Take out $3.50		– $3.50	$63.50
Put in $11.75	+ $11.75		$75.25
Put in $45.00	+ $45.00		$120.25
Put in $7.10	+ 7.10		$127.35
Take out $3.00		– $3.00	$124.35
Put in $8.50	+ $8.50		$132.85
Put in $16.40	+ $16.40		$149.25
Take out $12.25		– $12.25	$137.00
Put in $5.05	+ $5.05		$142.05
Ending balance			$142.05

$77.05

Raising Money to Help Others

1.

Food	Price	How many for one family?	Total cost for one family
turkey	$20.25	1	$20.50
can of green beans	$1.50	3	$4.50
bag of potatoes	$3.75	2	$7.50
can of cranberry sauce	$2.50	2	$5.00
bag of rolls	$6.00	1	$6.00
pie	$7.75	2	$15.50

2. $59.00
3. $531.00
4. $347.00

Planning a Party

Starting a Business

Page 95

entrepreneur; product; consumers; employee; risk; expenses; profit

Page 98

1. $7.50
2. 3 hours
3. $20.25
4. $432.00

Page 99

Job	Earned	Spent		Profit?
		Supplies	Employees	
1	$30.50	$18.75	$0	yes
2	$48.75	$19.25	$30.50	no
3	$100.00	$86.50	$10.25	yes
4	$53.75	$24.75	$22.25	yes
5	$78.25	$39.25	$39.50	no
6	$35.00	$17.00	$16.75	yes
7	$65.00	$0	$72.50	no
Total	$411.25	$205.50	$191.75	yes

Paying Bills

Page 107

Page 110

1. $105.00
2. $41.25
3. $132.25
4. $45.00

Page 111

1. $111.75
2. $229.70
3. $49.65
4. $19.25

Using Credit Cards

Paying for Health Services

STEAM
Project-Based Learning

GRADES 1-6

Real-World Learning for Tomorrow's Leaders!

STEAM is an approach to project-based learning that uses **Science, Technology, Engineering, the Arts, and Mathematics** to engage children in empathizing, thinking critically, collaborating, and coming up with solutions to solve real-world problems.

Each robust unit in this classroom resource focuses on a hands-on STEAM project that encourages students to enjoy the journey of creating and sharing his or her solutions to help create a better world.

128 reproducible pages.
Correlated to current standards.

Grade 3

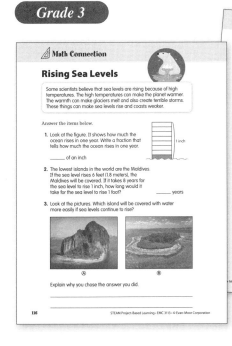

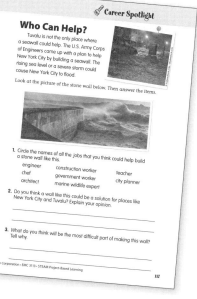

Teacher's Edition*

Grade 1	EMC 3111
Grade 2	EMC 3112
Grade 3	EMC 3113
Grade 4	EMC 3114
Grade 5	EMC 3115
Grade 6	EMC 3116

Available in print and e-book

Weekly
Grades 1–6

Real-World Writing

Real-World Learning for Tomorrow's Leaders!

Help students explore real-world purposes for writing with activities that demonstrate thoughtful and effective writing strategies.

The **24 writing units** within *Weekly Real-World Writing* focus on six common writing purposes: **self-expression, information, evaluation, inquiry, analysis, and persuasion.**

Weekly activities include letters, journal entries, product opinions, advertisements, directions, interviews, and more!

Units are designed to fit into a weekly lesson plan and include:

- Teacher overview page
- A writing sample to model each skill
- Graphic Organizer for student notes
- Two writing tasks with response pages
- An extension activity

**128 reproducible pages.
Correlated to current standards.**

Teacher's Resource Book*

Grades 1–2	EMC 6077
Grades 3–4	EMC 6078
Grades 5–6	EMC 6079

*Available in print and e-book

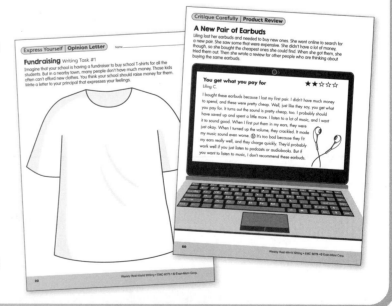

Grade 3